Bicycle Diaries

Bicycle Diaries

40 Days Around the Coast
of a Changing Ireland

Paul Shannon

Galley Head Press

First published in 2006 by Galley Head Press, Ardfield, Co. Cork
www.galleyheadpress.com

ISBN: 0 9542159 6 6

Typesetting: Dominic Carroll, Co. Cork
Printing: ColourBooks, Dublin

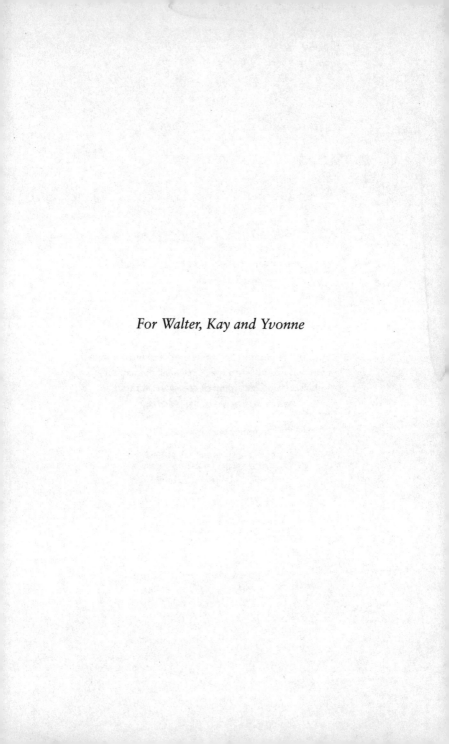

For Walter, Kay and Yvonne

Coleraine library is packed today. They must be avid readers here, or perhaps the heavy rain has something to do with it. I'm standing in a queue of a dozen or so people waiting to collect my computer printout from the librarian. I'm third in a line of what looks like a grumpy mixture of students, tourists, pensioners and a few lads afraid of a day's work. I think we're all feeling a bit annoyed because of that young fellow at the counter who's now wasted five minutes rummaging through his backpack in search of his library card.

I've spent the last hour surfing the Net in search of the IRA's statement declaring the end of the armed struggle. Those analysts who predicted its release today – 28 July 2005 – were spot on. I found it on the BBC website only minutes ago, hot off the press, so to speak. I'm anxious to study the details of what I know to be an historic declaration.

'Yes?' whispers the woman behind the counter, raising her chin in my direction.

'I've a printout to collect, please.'

'Sorry?' she says, only louder. This is not the first time my Cork accent has generated puzzlement. A lot of people can't make it out. I point to the printer, which at that moment spews out photographs of a Britney Spears lookalike.

'Are these yours?' she asks, without bothering to mask her disapproval.

1

'Not those, no. Below them. The printout from the BBC.'

'Say again,' she says, louder still.

'The – printout – from – the – BBC. Not – the – photographs.'

Now it's the turn of those behind me to start fidgeting. Someone towards the back of the queue appoints himself spokesman. 'Christ, will he ever hurry up. He's holding up the whole show.'

'What's written on it?' she shouts.

Now I've lost the rag. 'It's the one about the feckin' IRA!'

Away in the remotest corner of the library, a pin can be heard crashing to the floor.

The rain eases off as I push my bike down Millburn Road into Anderson Park and towards the Phoenix Peace Fountain in the rose garden. The crow picking on a half-eaten sandwich reminds me that I haven't eaten since breakfast. I can't say I'm one for monuments, but I'm impressed with this one – a gift in 2002 from what they like to call 'the communities of the United States' to 'the communities of Northern Ireland' as a symbol of the violence each has endured. A large phoenix emerges from a flaming nest to represent the North arising from the ashes of conflict. What makes it different to the dozens of other monuments I've seen around the island is that hundreds of guns were melted down to create it. The weapons were collected in America over a year, many of them having been used in hold-ups, murders and suicides. Outlines of the weapons in the nest section and at the base of the pool are clearly discernible. It's eerie to imagine that bits of this monument might have been used to take someone's life.

It seems like a good moment to read the IRA statement, so I sit on the black base of the fountain and take the printout from my pocket. 'The leadership of Óglaigh na hÉireann has formally ordered an end to the armed campaign.' All IRA volunteers are ordered to dump arms by four o'clock today.

I knew it was coming, but to actually see it in black and white is a bit surreal. I'm sure it'll come as a shock to many a man who fought to end partition – to some of them, a betrayal – but I sincerely hope it's another step in the direction of meaningful peace, and perhaps a step towards a United Ireland.

The timing of the statement is of special interest to me. As well as being an historic day in the sad and sorry history of my country, it's also the twenty-third day of my 'United Ireland' bicycle trip. I left Clonakilty in County Cork just over three weeks ago at the start of a coastline tour of Ireland, during which I've quizzed those I've met along the way about the prospect of a United Ireland. Do they want it? Will it happen? When? I'm not exactly conducting a nationwide poll, but I think I'm gaining an insight into current thinking about an age-old question. And learning something about this changing country of ours.

Day 1

I hardly slept a wink last night with the excitement of getting underway. On an overcast summer's morning, I head west from Clonakilty out the Skibbereen road. The next time I see Clon, I'll have cycled the entire coastline of Ireland, full circle. Along the way I plan to camp wherever I can – on beaches, in woods, fields, picnic spots, front lawns and the odd night in a garda station. I'll feast my eyes on rugged coastline, magnificent cliffs, sandy beaches and islands, while averting my gaze from holiday villages, super quarries and the occasional shantytown housing homesick Turkish road builders on less than the minimum wage. I'll savour country pubs with traditional music and *craic*, city pubs with rave music and crack, thatched-roof cottages, open bogland and slate-toned lakes. The musings of highly intelligent Americans, staunch republicans and die-hard unionists will keep boredom at bay, and all on €20 a day. I'm not a tight bastard – I just like the challenge. If money gets tight, mugging and bank robbery (especially up north) are always an option.

My iron donkey has been my trusty companion for many an expedition, through the west coast of America, the Hawaiian islands, Tahiti, the highways and byways of New Zealand, and on a 7,000-kilometre trek across the Australian desert. I bought it in a tiny shop in Dordrecht, Holland four years ago, never imagining the places it would take me to. I'm kitted out with four panniers, a tent, sleeping bag, stove, dictaphone, camcorder, still camera, clothes and a puncture-repair kit.

I'm ready for anything or anyone. My luxury item is a shortwave radio fixed to my handlebars. On boring sections, I'm sure it'll stop me from talking to myself or put some catchy tune in my head, and – most importantly – keep me informed as to the whereabouts of the WMDs.

The first mile seems to go on forever. Only 1,799 left on a trip that could well involve a few hundred pints of Guinness and God only knows how many punctures. The road is your typical Irish secondary route; not the winding, narrow type with grass up the middle, or the wide, busy-highway type, but something in between: a cross between a cow path and the road out of Baghdad. It's barely wide enough for two-way traffic, has yellow lines either side (the meaning of which I've never figured out), potholes to drive the saddle halfway up your arse, blind corners to enable boy-racers put the fear of God into you, and crossroads where nobody knows who has right of way. The signs of course are no help, but do add to the charm of getting lost.

The terrain here is fairly flat, with rolling countryside, farms and the odd pub popping up in the middle of nowhere. The ditches are thick with grass and adorned with tiny white, yellow and purple flowers and the odd plastic bag. Happy birds flit from hedge to hedge, and curious cows stare at me over galvanised gates.

My new speedometer tells me I'm travelling at 120 kilometres per hour. Great stuff! I'll be back in Clon tomorrow morning. It's not long before I realise that my luxury item is the source of the problem. Speedometers and radios hate the sight of each other. They're not married or anything, it's just that the magnet on the speakers interferes with the reading on the clock. They need to be separated. After pulling over by the mustard-yellow Pike Bar, I get out my toolkit and change the position of the speedometer. Problem solved. A photograph of the gaudy pub is officially the first photograph of my trip, but Christ, I can't believe I'm even thinking about having a pint this early in the day. Pedal on, pedal on.

I'm in the heart of an area that back in the Twenties was known to the Black and Tans as 'Bandit Country'. This rebellious region of Ireland was the scene of many an ambush of British soldiers and murderous pound-a-day mercenaries by the young lads of the Flying Columns. As I pedal along, I picture a dozen or so west Cork boys in battle-worn trench coats taking on the British Empire. 'Rat-a-tat-tat-tat' go the Lewis machine guns, before the lads melt away into the lush countryside on a misty morning.

At the end of a handy climb, I'm rewarded with panoramic views of the pretty village of Rosscarbery overlooking a sandy lagoon. Colourful town houses cluster around the village square, and the church steeple towers high above them all, like a rocket about to be launched into space. Beyond the village, rolling hills are dotted with trees resembling healthy bunches of broccoli. 'Forty Shades of Green' springs to mind, and I know I'll spend the next few hours trying to kick Mr Cash out of my head. I cross over the causeway that traverses the lagoon while watching herons in search of lunch. My magic moment is brought to a sudden halt when the bloody chain snaps. Christ! I can't believe it! I'm not an hour into the trip and it's already falling apart. After cursing and swearing for a few minutes, I tackle the broken chain with my tools and the spare links that only hours ago I was going to leave behind because I thought I'd never use them. I'm not a good mechanic so the job takes ages.

Job done. The babywipes come in handy for rubbing the

black oil from my hands, nose and forehead. But I'm in a pissed-off mood now and in no form to ask the people of Rosscarbery if they yearn for a thirty-two-county republic. Instead, I continue west for Skibbereen.

Arriving in the village of Leap, I spot a middle-aged man in no particular hurry, and I push my bike across the road with a view to asking him his views on a United Ireland.

'Christ, come here now boy, you're not looking for money are ye?' says he, after I've blocked his path.

I fill him in on the bike trip and he relaxes a bit. When I tell him I'm doing a bit of research on the national question, he jumps back with an angry stare – madness in his eyes, like I slept with his wife or something. 'Go on away now, fuck off with yourself. Ye shagging Provos have this country destroyed.'

The sky is clearing as I freewheel down the hill through the rest of the tiny village. The rough patch of road at the bottom knocks off my speedometer. After pulling myself out of a pothole, I pick up my little piece of technology and slap on some sunscreen.

Skibbereen is forever associated with the Famine that decimated nineteenth-century Ireland. The event is recalled by the famous song, 'Dear Old Skibbereen', which tells the story of a family evicted from their cottage by an English landlord, who sets the roof on fire. The mother dies on the snowy ground and is buried in a pauper's grave, while her husband and children emigrate to America for a better life. Not unnaturally, hatred for the English spawned rebellion, and a monument in Skibb honours those who did the fighting and serves as a reminder of the strong feelings still alive in west Cork.

The Eldon Hotel in the main street claims to have served Michael Collins his last meal before he was shot in Béal na mBláth in 1922. But the townsfolk of Bandon will spin you a different story. 'In Skibb? Are ye joking me or what, boy! Sure, didn't he have it here in the Munster Arms Hotel.'

Ironically, this once unfortunate town has now declared itself the luckiest place in Ireland, with more people becoming lottery millionaires here than anywhere else in the country. Needless to say, I pop into a corner shop and do a Quick-Pick for tonight's draw. Wish me luck.

Eager to get going again, I leave the Lotto capital behind me, and head for the village of Ballydehob, only twenty-odd kilometres from Mizen head. Forgive me for hopping from miles to kilometres and back again, but that's the way we're doing it in Ireland at the moment. It was only in January that the speed limits were changed from miles to kilometres, but phrases like 'Dublin, sure that's fecking kilometres away' or 'Ah sure, it's only down the road a few kilometres' have yet to catch on.

The road to Ballydehob is an easy, flat one, and the superior quality of the surface is kilometres ahead of anything I've experienced anywhere else on earth [sarcasm]. Roads like this make me glad I spent the extra few euro on the suspension, but I'll have to spend a few more on ointments.

I cross over small stone bridges, and pass old churches, a dead hedgehog and the ruins of cottages buried in ivy. It's a lonely road at times, but the odd car that passes gives me loads of room.

I'm starving when I arrive in the little village of Ballydehob. Craving a sandwich, I make a purchase of cheese, tomatoes and a sliced pan in the small shop on the main street, and find a quiet picnic spot down beneath an old railway bridge overlooking the river. It hasn't seen a train since the Fifties, and now the twelve-arched stone structure serves as a walkway for locals and tourists. As I ponder the still waters, I'm approached by a middle-aged Australian couple, who, I quickly learn, are driving around Ireland in search of the headstones of their relatives. Ian and Margaret are from Perth. She left Ireland when she was only fourteen, and is a quiet, laid-back woman with a gentle tone that still bears the Irish lilt. He's your typical straight-up, no-holds-barred Aussie, with a wild, dingo-like laugh. I think the issue of a United Ireland is really for the Irish alone to consider, but I put the question to them just for the hell of it. 'Don't really know,' says Ian, 'but I do think religion will have to disappear from the island before anything else happens, and as that'll never happen, I suppose there'll never be a United Ireland.'

Margaret is only slightly more optimistic. 'It *will* happen – I hope it does – but not in my lifetime.'

As they take off in their little red Fiat to find her great-grandfather's grave somewhere near Durrus, I finish off my fourth sandwich. Cycling really works up an appetite.

At the west end of the village, I gaze on the lifesize statue of the wrestler Danno Mahony, aka 'The Irish Whip'. Built like a bear, Danno crossed the Atlantic back in the Thirties and fought his way to the world championship at a time when wrestling was still a sport, not pantomime. Judging by his stance, he's still up for a fight. These bronze commemorative statues have popped up all over the country these past few years, and I'm sure I'll see many more along the way. An American couple ask me to take their photo with Danno. Texans to a fault, they're nevertheless proud of being third-generation Irish. But though they've come to Ireland every year, they won't be coming again 'because things have gone so Goddamn expensive.'

The rugged landscape of the Mizen Peninsula is sparsely populated, but quite a few tourists are out walking the roads. Most of the houses around here have either 'B+B' or 'For Sale' signs outside them. Whether it's evidence of good times or bad, I'm not quite sure. Before Schull, the inland view is dominated by the 400-metre Mount Gabriel and its famous golfball-like radar station scanning the south coast. The INLA blew a hole in it back in 1982, claiming it was being used by NATO in breach of Ireland's neutrality. No doubt it was. Nowadays, our famed neutrality must seem something of a joke to the American soldiers gracing the lounges of Shannon Airport (aka Warport) en route to the quagmire in Iraq. Still, the duty-free is raking it in, as many a Fianna Fáil politician keeps reminding us.

The tiny fishing village of Schull has become a Mecca for watersports enthusiasts, arty types, well-to-do Brits and the trendy set. Cycling up the main street, I could just as easily be in the south of France. The punters relaxing at drink-laden tables outside pubs and restaurants soak up the sun whilst sporting the coolest of sunshades. Murphy Irish Stout signs plead with me to stop and sup. But it's approaching six, so I put my head down and keep her lit, as we say. I've a few more miles yet before I reach Mizen Head.

The road to Goleen – along what's called the bog road – immediately turns inland and remains so for much of my journey, except for a magic, coast-hugging section through the tiny, blink-if-you-miss-it, cove village of Toormore. The odd little boat is tied offshore, hidden in the bushes at the edge of the bay, and the pace of life is on its lowest setting. Goleen itself is a small, wide-street village built on a crossroads at the tip of one of the remotest parts of Ireland. It's easy to conjure up images of donkeys and carts going to market and men in tweed caps discussing the price of cattle back in olden days, but today it's not much different to any other village you'd see in west Cork. The thing that really strikes me is the community spirit. People blow their horns, wave at each other, stop to chat on the street, have the *craic* in the shop. Everybody knows everybody, and even before I leave the small shop with a litre of water, three people ask me how I'm getting on. I'm used to this friendliness after growing up in a village in Cork, but it must be an amazing experience for foreigners not used to the eye contact and a friendly 'Hello' as you walk down the street. My years abroad have made me appreciate simple things like this even more, and it all brings a smile to my face. My smile broadens even wider when I discover I'm able to get an Indian meal in a takeaway next door. Who'd have thought it a few years ago? Indian food in Goleen. I sit by the window eating hot curry and read my map as the street outside begins to fill with youngsters fuelling up on burger and chips in readiness for a busy Wednesday night.

According to the map there are two routes to Mizen Head: the direct, cross-county route would be quickest, but I think I'll stick to the coast. The tip of the peninsula is less then five miles away and I've at least two hours of daylight left.

The road wraps itself along the coastline with only a low stonewall separating me from the bay. The village of Crookhaven appears across the water at the edge of a finger of land pointing eastwards. As the crow flies, it seems about half a mile across the water. The houses are a riot of colour, and numerous small sailboats with long masts cling to orange buoys as they bob up and down in a random fashion across the inlet. It's appealing, but it's not on my route. I'll be faced with many options of side trips like this to wonderful places like Crookhaven, but I have to be realistic. If I take the side-trip option every time it crops up, it'll take years to encircle the country.

The apex of the inlet is lined with a narrow sandy beach strewn with seaweed, and a few brightly dressed people are out for an evening stroll. The natural beauty of the landscape is scarred by an unnatural caravan park. If only these monstrosities were obliged to camouflage themselves with foliage or sand dunes.

I'm only a speck on the landscape as I freewheel down towards Barley Cove – an estuary dotted with sand dunes, salt marshes, streams and lagoons. A hotel complex dominates the western side, overlooking what's known as Ocean Beach. Couples walk hand in hand and playfully push each other. It's a good place to be in love.

The road out of the cove is steep and testing. This day has taken its toll on my legs, but I'm close to the top. I push hard. Maybe too hard, because the chain snaps again. Christ! I've a good mind to catch the bike and fuck it in over the ditch and watch it sink into the ocean.

The road here is way too narrow to attempt repairs, so I push the bike up the rest of the hill and find a gravel patch outside a house. As my body cools down, I realise just how cold an evening it is. My hands grow numb, and it's hard to connect the chain links. A few tourists out for a walk – they're from Cork, judging by their accents – show no interest in my plight as they hasten their step. I'd be the first to help someone out in a situation like this, and in some of the other countries I've cycled in, people would at least be polite enough to ask if you're alright.

My sense of despair deepens when I discover the chain link I have is faulty. I kneel on the gravel while contemplating my black hands and the oily chain, and wonder what the hell I'm going to do. Deep in thought, I hear a soft voice. 'Are you OK? Do you need help?' As if in a dream, a beautiful woman in her twenties – tall and blonde – stares at me from within the fluffy sheepskin collar of her suede jacket. She's Dutch, I can tell. Having assured her that I'm fine – even though I'm not – I attempt some friendly conversation with her, but she's not having any of it and quickly disappears down the hill. Bollocks. Still, her kindness has put me in better form, and I get to work filing down the faulty link.

The sun has turned orange by the time I get the chain back on. The gears are jumping a bit, but at least I'm on the move again. A mile or so later I arrive at the red-and-white Mizen

Head Visitor Centre. It's closed and there's not a sinner in sight. A mural on a gable depicts the long white bridge that crosses the sea to a sheer-faced rocky island upon which the signal station proudly stands. I can only assume they felt the need to illustrate the very scene I'm looking at for the occasions when fog casts its cloak of invisibility over the real thing. Whatever the reason, I intend to cross that bridge high above the churning Atlantic first thing in the morning.

With the light fading fast, my only option for camping is the field adjacent to the visitors' centre. I sling my bike and gear over a gate and onto the grassy slope close to the cliffs. I set up my tent in no time. It's one of those fast-and-light jobbies, so you'd do it blindfolded. By the time I get a pot of water boiling on my stove, the night has turned pitch black. Grasping a steaming cup of tea, I follow the lights of passing ships and reflect on my first day. I boil another pot of water for my sponge bath, then hit the sack. Perched on the most south-westerly point of the country, I drift off to sleep to the lullaby of an Atlantic breeze.

Day 2

I'm woken up by what sounds like a helicopter landing not far from my tent. It's panic stations as I struggle to free myself from the sleeping bag. A quick peep reveals one of those verge-cutting tractors that trim the ditches, and not the Irish Army preparing to whisk me off on an extraordinary-rendition exercise. Phew!

But now I think it might be the local farmer, and that might mean a 'Who's been camping in my field' confrontation. I quickly pack my tent, gather my gear and throw everything onto the road. If the farmer says anything, I'll just pretend I'm a German tourist with brutal bad English. Luckily, it turns out to be a guy from the County Council.

The Mizen Head Visitor Centre won't open till ten, so I take the opportunity to sort out the gears of my bike. I've come to the conclusion that the chain and gear cable are shagged. That's not the worse problem though, because the cassette on the rear wheel has seen better days – in fact, it's totally worn. Chain and cable I can afford, but not a new cassette. The front brakepads have also been giving trouble – they were screeching a lot yesterday because of a bent disc blade – so I remove them. I'll still have loads of braking power but I'm concerned that the rear pads will wear faster. All these problems waited until I was on the road to reveal themselves, of course, but I suppose all the extra weight is putting additional stress on the various mechanical parts.

There's quite a bit of construction work going on around the centre this morning. Several lads dressed in yellow high-visibility vests are hammering away. I've spent the last few years abroad, and I've noticed since returning a new safety consciousness on building sites – a good thing, too. Gone are the days we poured concrete barefoot.

A Spanish tourist appears from nowhere. He's from Barcelona, he says, and is staying at the hotel back down the road. He tells me his name but I've already forgotten it as he pronounces it. As I continue with running repairs, he surveys the centre, then becomes flustered and tells me it's closed for the day because of construction. Gutted, I throw the bags onto the bike and start walking back towards Goleen. The Spaniard walks alongside, but the pace is slow and the poor man is a bit boring, so I hop aboard and wave adiós.

The weather is superb – the kind of day when you can see for miles. I switch on my radio to hear what's happening in the world. The news is confusing. No-one's sure yet, but it seems bombs have just gone off in the London Underground. Lots of people killed. They think it's an Al-Qaeda attack. More madness.

Memories from the morning of 9/11 come flooding back. I was living in San Francisco and watched it all unfold on

15

CNN. But I can't say I'm surprised to hear that London is under attack – it was surely only a matter of time. If you send in your army, as Blair did, and annihilate thousands of Iraqis, something's got to give. It's tragic, though, that innocent Londoners have to pay the price. By the time I get to Goleen, one of London's famous double-deckers has exploded.

I find a bench and commence my breakfast of muesli and milk from a saucepan, much to the amusement of the locals. I'm kind of amused myself at how so many of them are sitting around in cars for no apparent reason. All is revealed when the local postman arrives and delivers mail directly to the occupants of the cars, taking time to have a quick chat with each one. Never seen this done before.

I'm clearing up my breakfast when curiosity gets the better of Pat – that's his name, he tells me – who gets straight down to the first of his 101 questions. He's not local – somewhere from the east coast I'd say. The London bombs are discussed, and I'm impressed with how he connects today's incident with the question I put to him about a United Ireland. 'Well, with all that shite happening in London this morning, it shows again how England always reaps what she sows.' He reckons that the day there'll be a United Ireland is the day England will know what the word 'respect' means. 'That'll probably never happen, so we may never see a thirty-two-county Ireland.'

It's quarter-past-one when I reach the famous anchor monument on the edge of Bantry. This enormous relic was found during a trawl in Bantry Bay in 1964, and is believed to be from the French fleet that sailed into the bay in 1796 at the behest of Wolfe Tone to assist the United Irishmen in their bid for freedom. I wonder how things would have worked out if the weather had been kinder to them and allowed them to land at Bantry. Would there be a United Ireland today?

Bantry holds many good memories for me: days on pub

crawls with friends, sharing freshly cooked mussels with tourists, watching The Chieftains and Mary Black play live in the square on the back of a lorry as my pint of stout fills up with rain. And a few less memorable ones of trying to hitch a ride home at four in the morning.

The focal point of town is Wolfe Tone Square, nestled between the colourful town buildings and Bantry harbour. The yellow-brick square taking up close to a half an acre is a cold and uncomplementary addition to the town. I like the monuments of Wolfe Tone and St Brendan, but this low-maintenance brick monstrosity has as much character as a slab of concrete. Where's the green grass and the colourful flower beds?

I push my bike down the yellow-brick road to the tourist information centre where hopefully the Wizard of Oz will tell me where I can get my bike fixed. A young girl behind the counter (probably Dorothy) directs me to Nigel's bikeshop.

Nigel is a thin man in his forties. He has wild black hair, oily hands and speaks with an English accent. He tells me he's up the walls and has a load of stuff to get finished, but manages to find time to sell me a new chain, a cable and a few spare links, and even gives me advice about my rear cassette.

Leaving the bustling, unengaging town of Bantry behind me, I head north along the busy N71, eventually swinging west towards Glengarriff. This stretch is very testing, and the ups and downs quickly tire me. Views of Bantry Bay, Whiddy Island and the distant Caha Mountains on the Beara Peninsula offer respite, and I eventually reach the last major climb before a sweeping descent into the village.

The tourist hub of Glengarriff is jointed with happy couples sitting at tables outside pubs, hill-walkers strutting their stuff, packs of noisy bikers shining their Harley's, exhausted cyclists stretching their hamstrings, and husbands sitting in cars having a fag out the window, waiting for the wife to come back with the ice-creams. It's as good a spot as anywhere in the world right now, and I treat myself to a cone.

Heading west out of Glengarriff along the R572, I embark on the scenic route known as the Ring of Beara. The Beara Peninsula is split between the counties of Cork and Kerry, with the mighty Caha Mountains running down the spine of the peninsula. The road I'll take will hug the edge of the peninsula all the way to Kenmare, over a hundred kilometres away. I know it'll be a hard slog because I've been this way before in a car.

My handy start counts for nothing when three kilometres down the road a substantial climb begins up the side of the Sugarloaf Mountain. It's a fairly steep grade, but spectacular views unfold of this rugged, rock-studded landscape and the craggy fingers of rock poking into Bantry Bay. The odd mussel farm dots the blue water. There are few signs of habitation here beyond the odd farmhouse nestled between the rocks and hedges.

At the small harbour village of Adrigole, a huge pint of Murphy's stout painted on the gable of Thady's Bar fails to break my rhythm. Views of Bere Island just off the coast and Hungry Hill to my right keep me going until I roll into the sleepy fishing town of Castletownbere at seven-thirty. The town is quiet tonight, but I know from my visits here before that the port is fierce busy during the day with the hustle and bustle of one of Ireland's largest fishing fleets. After crossing the Brandy Hall Bridge into town, I stop at a seated area overlooking the narrow stretch of water between the mainland and Bere Island. It's peaceful here, with not a puff of wind. I watch a bunch of brown-and-black ducks paddling around a bright-blue rowing boat rocking on the still water..What a life these ducks have – not a care in the world. One of them is blowing his nose; I think the poor bird might have flu.

I glance at the commemorative bust of Timothy Harrington

(1851–1910), lord mayor of Dublin in the early 1900s and secretary of the National League. 'His name will go down to posterity as one of the noblest Irishmen that ever lived' proclaims the inscription. Can't say I know a whole pile about the man, so posterity must have a short memory.

Castletownbere doesn't hold me long. A few minutes outside town, I stop to have a chat with two donkeys and a huge brown-and-white horse (the head off Boxer in *Animal Farm*) incarcerated behind an electric fence. Cheltenham and the price of hay dominates the conversation, and I have to answer the usual 'Where do you sleep?' and 'How many punctures do you get?' questions.

A long gradual climb out of the valley gives me a bird's-eye view west to Dursey Island and Kenmare Bay. I turn north at the tip of the peninsula and head for the famous village of Allihies. By the time I climb the last hill into the village, I'm a wreck. But this is rocky, remote Ireland as Hollywood likes to portray it. Nestled against a craggy backdrop, it gives you an edge-of-the-world feeling. Pedalling through the village, I catch the music drifting from the pubs. Resisting its lure is not easy, but it's approaching ten o'clock and I'm anxious to find a camping spot before it gets too dark. A few miles from the village – as I'm beginning to fret about finding somewhere suitable – I stumble on a perfect site hidden from the road. Sure, it's perched on the edge of a cliff overlooking the frothing ocean, but I only have to remember not to sleepwalk.

Day 3

On a beautiful Beara morning, I share an apple with an old hairy donkey on the side of the road to Urhan. Not much in Urhan to be honest, and getting here has been brutal hard. But in all fairness, this road has got to be one of the most dramatic coastal routes in the entire world. I've travelled thousands of miles of coastline across the globe and have a lot to compare it with, but the Beara setting is unique and awe-inspiring stuff.

All morning I've been craving a good fry-up – a good greasy Irish breakfast. It's a mad kind of obsession that makes me feel like a heroine addict, and I'm elated to stumble across a shop at the side of the road – it's actually a little house masquerading as a shop, and is not unlike a museum – and I'm impressed by the sheer quantity of stuff the owner has managed to squash into it: DIY stuff, posh toiletries and fresh fruit are all heaped together. The shopkeeper is a broad lady in her sixties, very friendly and helpful, a real country girl. I had a plan of what I wanted when I walked into the shop two seconds ago, but now the clutter of stuff has made my mind go blank. What's my name again? The sight of half a pound of sausages in the little fridge refreshes my memory. Paul – yes, that's my name. I'm cycling around Ireland. I want a fry.

The easiest way to shop here is to ask the woman for everything. She knows where it all is, and it'll save me a few hours. As the tomatoes are being loaded into a wispy plastic bag, the stack of newspapers on the counter catches my eye. '07/07/05' is emblazoned on the front pages in thick black writing, together with the image of a ripped-apart London bus. We talk about the events of yesterday and what it may lead to. She wishes me luck on the trip and assures me that the road to Kenmare is not nearly as hilly as the one I've just travelled on from Allihies.

In Eyeries, I bump into an old classmate – Fintan. I haven't seen him for years. He's driving a fruit-and-veg van, doing deliveries along the peninsula. Married with a kid, he tells me he's built a house in Bandon. He's come a long way from the days we used to do the bollox on the back of the bus going to school in Dunmanway.

I'm in Ardgroom before I know it, and I notice Fintan's van. Somewhere around Kilmakilloge Harbour, I stop at the side of the road and cook a massive fry-up with eggs, black pudding and half a pound of sausages.

Kenmare's Irish name, 'An Neidín', means 'The Little Nest' – appropriate, as the small town nestles on the seashore between the Cork and Kerry mountains. It's a riot of colour here, and the shop signs are artistic and tasteful, unlike the Kerry GAA jerseys sported by the local lads in anticipation of their team kicking Cork's ass in the Munster Final next Sunday. 'C'mon on the Rebels,' I shout to one youngster attired in the full Kerry kit. He face has disgust written all over it, but otherwise he's stuck for a response. I fear his answer may come next Sunday.

I need to do some bulk shopping here, as I won't see a cheap supermarket for days, but my empty wallet needs replenishment from an ATM. I withdraw €60.

A farmer-type – arms folded and resting on the bonnet of a car – catches my eye. 'God Almighty! But you've got some load on that fucking thing there,' says he.

'Ah well, it's not too bad when you get used to it, I suppose,' says I.

In his thirties, he's dressed like a man in his sixties. Learning I'm from Cork, he gives a dig about the match, and adds that if I'm in town next week, I won't be so 'fucking chirpy'. His wife, he informs me, is a shopaholic who insists on calling to every boutique in town to satisfy her cravings, so once a week he takes up his usual position in the square, on his bonnet, awaiting her return. 'Christ, 'twas fine when I was on

21

the beer waiting in the pub all day, but that fucking doctor took me off it, so now I have to stay out here, playing with myself till the fucking bitch comes back. The ol' cow'll have to learn to drive, that's all there is to it!' His teeth, like his foul language, are rotten. If the farming fails him, I'm sure The Pogues might fit him in somewhere. I wonder what his considered view of the vexed question of a United Ireland might be.

'Oh ho! You can be fucking sure of it, boy. We'll breed those fuckers out of it up there, yet. When that happens, we'll get back what those Orange fuckers stole from us.'

I stock up on supplies, and pedal over a tiny bridge to begin the Ring of Kerry – a tourist trail of around 175 kilometres that cuts around the Iveragh Peninsula. It officially begins in Killarney, but I want to keep my sanity, so I'll avoid that magnet for tourists. Outside Kenmare, I take the N70 to my left. With the first few kilometres consisting of fields and forests, I soon find myself bumping along the roughest road in Ireland. To be fair, the road is currently under construction, and I don't expect the rest of my trip in Kerry to involve dodging knocked-down orange cones. Judging by the total absence of workers, my guess is that the council is doing the job.

I take on liquid refreshment at Pat Spillane's Bar. Pat is a bit of a football legend throughout the country, after winning eight All-Ireland medals for Kerry. He's retired from football and is teaching in a school in Bantry, so thankfully he won't be playing on Sunday.

It's late in the evening now and traffic is quiet. The odd car whizzes by and I can't but feel a great sense of gratitude for my mode of transport. I can hear, see and feel my surroundings. I put out my hand and touch the long grass as I pedal by. I pity those seeing a fifty-miles-an-hour blurred image through a pane of glass. Get a bike and smell life. I suppose I should keep that secret to myself though or I'll soon be sharing the beautiful Kerry roads with thousands of cyclists. I rented a bike in Beijing years ago and almost drowned in a river of bicycles. I towered above everybody as I pedalled down the middle of an expanse of black-haired Chinese. They seemed amused at the sight of a big awkward Paddy with pale, freckled legs pedalling alongside them through the smoggy streets. The fun started when I wanted to turn left. But trapped in the midst of a moving ant colony, I hadn't a hope in hell. Within a few days, though, I had learnt the art of cycling in Beijing, and by the end of the week I was a pro. Now, years later, I can still hear the millions of bicycle bells ringing in my ears.

Far from Beijing, and not a Chinaman in sight, I arrive in the pretty village of Sneem. Lying on the estuary of the River Sneem, its Irish name translates as 'Knot' – hence its nickname 'The Knot in the Ring'. It's after nine, and I'm anxious to camp up for the night. I ask for directions from an elderly man sat in his little black car with the door wide open. I'd guess he's in his seventies, and his fingers are bright yellow from years of smoking. His index finger has an abnormally long nail, and he constantly rubs the chin of his hardened face with it.

'Have ye a tent?' says he.

'I have, yea.'

'Well sure, can't ye camp on the green there. Nobody'll say nothing to ya.'

I'm not so sure, and I pause in the square for a few minutes whilst contemplating whether or not I should halt here for the night. A bunch of rowdy Dutchmen gathered outside a bar turn me off the idea.

Just outside the village an elderly man is hitchhiking and waves me down. 'Jasus. Where are you off to at this hour of the night?' he asks, whilst struggling to stay upright.

'I'm just going out of town to look for somewhere to camp.'

'Ah well, there's no shortage of fields out there anyway. You

23

know, I might end up staying there myself, with the luck I'm having tonight.'

He asks me how far I've cycled and I end up telling him all about the trip.

'Ask me the question – go on,' he says, suddenly standing up straight and composing himself.

'Alright so. Do you think there'll ever be a United Ireland?'

'Well, do you know something, I'd like nothing better than to see a United Ireland. It's close, really close, but at my age I don't think I'll ever see it. God knows, but they've been fighting for it long enough and we all deserve a bit of peace. That's it really, I suppose. Well, be on your way now, and watch out for those blashted buses on the road – they'd flatten you and wouldn't even slow down!'

My search for a suitable site for the night is resumed, and I see hope in the distance in the form of a commercial forest perched on the side of a hill. A steel bar guards the entrance, but this is no Checkpoint Charlie, and I wander up the network of narrow roads that service the forest. Logs are scattered around, but there's been no activity here for years.

After setting up camp and cooking up some of Kenmare's finest frozen vegetables and rice, I take my pot and walk while I eat. It's a gorgeous summer's evening but light is quickly fading. Flocks of crows fly overhead, back to roost for the night. Midges develop a fascination for me, so I retreat to my fortress and zip up the doors. A bloody, five-minute battle is concluded with the death of dozens of my foes who had sneakily invaded while I was absent.

I've had far worse experiences with insects during my travels. In Brazil, I went hitchhiking in the Pantanal – the largest swampland in the world – and slept rough in a hammock with a built-in mosquito net. 'State of the art, sir,' the salesman in San Francisco had claimed. On the day my supply of repellent spray had been exhausted by some curious

24

Brazillians, I double-checked the mosquito net before nodding off. In the early hours, I suddenly awoke with the feeling that my skin was on fire. My back felt like braille from hundreds of bites. I searched for the little bleeders, and was puzzled not to find a single mosquito. Then the penny dropped: the little bastards had been drilling through the canvas of my hammock. I quickly discovered hundreds of well-fed mosquitos clinging to the canvas in anticipation of their next meal.

Later that day I got picked up by an off-duty chief of police in his fifty-year-old car. As I explained why I was sitting so awkwardly, an inch of ash fell from his cigar onto the mangy carpet as his body convulsed with laughter.

The wetland is home to animals like the jacaré – a crocodile – the anaconda and piranha fish, and the chief of police was even more amused when I told him how a capybara – the world's largest rodent – had whacked me as it ran under my hammock earlier that morning. And how an hour later, while fishing for a piranha with a piece of meat at the end of a hook, a jacaré jumped out of the muddy water, inches away, with my piece of meat in its mouth. With the line foolishly wrapped around my finger, it embarked on a death-roll, nearly pulling my finger off in the process. After a tug of war, I was able to release my finger and make good my escape. The policeman was still laughing when he dropped me off. Gringoes!

Back in my Irish jungle, I switch on my radio for the news. The London-bombing death-toll has risen to forty-nine and Hurricane Dennis is hitting Cuba hard. But it's not all bad news: George Bush fell off his bike at the G8 summit.

Day 4

Beara peninsula lies soft and dark in the distance. Below me, on a beautiful sandy beach, a petrol-guzzling 4x4 is being driven at speed. I search frantically for my rocket-propelled-grenade launcher, but seem to have left it at home. A stonewall serves as a table for my breakfast of left-overs from Urhan. My bike interests a middle-aged Italian who's pulled over to take some photos. He tells me I have a 'good life', and describes in detail his Italian-made Bianchi that now hangs on his living-room wall back in Milan. From his language, you'd think he was describing some sex goddess – a mechanical mistress – and his wife, perhaps jealous, retreats to the car, from where moments later she blows the horn. Like a well-heeled hound, he leaps into the motor, and they're off.

The village of Castle Cove – like every village in Ireland – has famous sons about whom it is justly proud. Memorial plaques displayed in the village refer to All-Ireland cycling and hop-skip-and-jump champions – a lovely reminder of the inter-village sports competitions long ago. Underneath the plaques, a large sheet of plywood – painted green and yellow – reads 'Best wishes from the Blackshop, to Declan & Jack & Kerry team.' They love their sport in this area, and why not?

As the day progresses, tour buses become more frequent. Near Glenbeg, a white sandy beach at the head of a half-moon bay plays host to holidaymakers. Children scamper on the rocks and adults paddle dinghies by the shore, but the caravans and mobile homes cheapen the landscape, much like a Mona Lisa with rotten teeth. A tricolour flutters high above the beach, as if to say 'This is Ireland and we love it.'

A tour bus pulls in beside me and a mixture of Germans and Dutch step out for a breath of fresh air or a fag. A middle-aged couple stop, point to my bike and begin speaking to me in Dutch. The look of puzzlement on my face is quickly understood, and the woman explains the confusion. 'Ah! You are not Dutch? We though you were when we saw your Dutch bicycle.'

They're from Amsterdam, and are impressed by the fact I had worked in the city for two years. The woman is less impressed with my failure to grasp even the rudiments of the Dutch language. She is somewhat astounded to hear that I lived in the Turkish part of The Hague, and tells me that the Turks and Moroccans are ruining her country. Apparently, they're responsible for everything bad in Holland.

Her male partner shakes his head in disagreement. I give him a smile and she winces. 'Must go,' I lie.

With Cahernageeha Mountain behind me, I sail into the beautiful village of Waterville. This gorgeous town lies on the shores of Ballinskelligs Bay, with Lough Currane to its rear. Its Irish name, 'An Coireán', means 'Little Whirlpool', and the village is basically a triangle of pubs, restaurants and shops, with a rocky beach that stretches for miles. I'm surprised to come across a statue of Charlie Chaplin, his famous walking stick in hand. Surely Charlie wasn't from Waterville? I learn that this was in fact one of his favourite holiday destinations, and that he spent many months of his life here. And I can't blame him.

Glorious sunshine bathes me as I savour a beautiful pint of Guinness. Conversation is struck up with a Swedish couple, and I ask them where the other half of ABBA is, but they're not impressed. Both seem a bit tipsy, which might have something to do with their membership of a Swedish club that travels to different parts of Europe to taste native beers. These two are real enthusiasts.

After my pint I cycle to the top of the street to stock up on whatever useful supplies can be purchased in Centra. It's aggravating to squander cash on bottled water, but tap-water is fast disappearing from Ireland. Growing up in west Cork, I remember taps on most streets, but they're all gone now.

These days, leave the house for more than an hour and you could flake out from dehydration. Is it a ploy to make us consume more Coca-Cola and Ballygowan?

I treat myself to a cone and a National Lottery scratch card. It's years since I bought a card, and as I scrunch it into a ball and toss it into a bin, it comes back to me why I haven't bothered for so long.

I jump on my iron donkey and head for the hills. Picturesque Waterville quickly recedes into the distance as I pedal north towards Cahirciveen. Until now, Cahirciveen has twice impressed itself upon my consciousness – though only once happily so. First, as the place where Daniel O'Connell – the Great Liberator – first saw the light of day, and then as the setting for the incredible saga of the 'Cahirciveen Baby'.

To those who don't know – and there are more and more of them in Ireland – let me first sketch a brief portrait of the man Dan. Born: 1775. Famous for: Catholic Emancipation. Died: Genoa, 1847. Cause of death: Broken Heart. Yes, it's true – Irish heroes have often succumbed to this ailment. Charles Stewart Parnell did, and so too did Oscar Wilde. I suspect that the same script will appear on the death cert of our disgraced former leader, Charles Haughey, when he finally croaks.

After Dan, there was Joanne. The 'fame' of Cahirciveen has endured owing to the sad episode of the 'Cahirciveen Baby'. Its little body was washed up on the White Strand, three miles from town. The year was 1984, and what followed was indeed Orwellian. After it was established that the baby had been stabbed to death, the police scoured the area for any recently pregnant woman who apparently had no baby to show for her efforts. The net closed around twenty-four-year-old Joanne Hayes, who admitted to having concealed a still-birth. With the help of her family, the little corpse had been buried on the farm in Abbeydorney, around thirty miles from Cahirciveen.

(Joanne's family had also hoped to bury the scandal of her having become pregnant through an affair with a married man – a local worthy, of course.) Joanne's admission was somewhat inconvenient for the police, who still needed a murderer to own up to the baby found in Cahirciveen. Unless … unless Joanne Hayes had twins (and for some inexplicable reason buried them thirty miles apart). Enter forensics: 'Sorry, inspector; two babies, different fathers.' Enter gung-ho detective with a copy of *New Scientist*: 'Superfecundation – that's what they call it. Two fathers, one pregnancy! Twins! The little vixen!' Now there was only the small matter of – ahem – extracting a confession for this darstadly – nay, ingenious – crime from Ms Hayes and family. The confession was duly extracted and Joanne was charged with murder.

The whole thing was so ludicrous it didn't even get to court. A public outcry led to a half-arsed enquiry, but the game was up for the cops. I was only twelve at the time, but well remember the impact the scandal had. It was a time in our history when the Garda Síochána – like the clergy – were still considered infallible, but only just, and the enquiry was one of the first challenges to their authority. Twenty years later – through an avalanche of revelation – no-one is in any doubt about the untrustworthyness of cops and priests, and bad eggs are being sniffed out with every passing day. Nasty.

Cahirciveen marks the halfway mark round the Ring of Kerry. The locals long ago proclaimed their village the capital of the Iveragh Peninsula, and it does have a welcoming feel to it. At the foot of the Beentee Mountains and beside the Fertha River, it's hard to beat the location. But I wouldn't fancy living here in a cold Irish winter. In the early 1800s there were reportedly only five houses here, but with a current population of around 1,500, a few more have been built since – many to the design of deranged 'architects', it goes without saying.

Tractors get in the way of cars and tour buses in an obvious

29

bid to ratchet up the rural charm, and the colourful street is packed with every kind of business intent on persuading the Yank to stay just long enough to part with a few dollars. I can't resist the fresh aroma of a traditional chip shop, and swap several euros for a crispy, fish-and-chip dinner. Outside, my petite table-and-chair ensemble looks as though it was liberated from a kindergarten, and my knees and elbows protrude into the ribs of oncoming pedestrians. My plate is bigger than the table, yet somehow I find room for my guidebook. Munching tasty cod, I flick the pages in search of a nearby wooded area or beach – somewhere suitable for the night. When a shadow descends over me, I look up to find a curious denizen of Cahirciveen casting a critical eye over my iron donkey.

'Having a good trip, are ye?' he asks.

'Oh yea! I'm having a mighty time, especially on a day like today.' To add emphasis, I wave my arm, and come dangerously close to knocking the head off a passing youngster.

Michael is in his early twenties, and is curious about my trip and my foreign travels. 'I'd love to go abroad and do a bit of travelling myself,' he tells me, 'but I just can't seem to get up and go. I've a good job and don't want to lose that either,' he says, unsure of his future. 'My friend Seán and myself are thinking of getting a twelve-month working visa for Australia,' he reveals.

I do my best to persuade him to go, but he's reluctant and I suspect he's something of a home-bird.

Before he rushes off to meet his friends in the pub, I ask him the burning question. There's a look of surprise on his face, as though the question had never before been put to him. 'Oh! You're after putting me on the spot there. Well … ahh … I think it has to happen sometime, but "when" is the question. I'd like to see it in the next ten to fifteen years. We should end partition now. Well, enough said!'

Contradictory, but telling.

It's after seven when I pedal away from Cahirciveen, but I pause momentarily to take a photograph of the monument depicting St Brendan sailing to America long, long, long before Christopher what's-his-name. (Yes ... if anyone 'discovered' it – anyone, that is, other than the natives already living there – it was us, not the Spaniards and not the Portuguese. But that's another story!)

Cycling east along the N70, I pedal a few ups and an equal number of downs, but mostly it's flat. To my left, a picture-postcard view of Dingle Bay comes into view. A low sun spreads its glow over the entire bay, and the green fields sweep down to the sea. The breathtaking spectacle leaves me with a deep appreciation for the country I was born in.

It's gone nine-thirty when I approach Glenbeigh village, and a caravan park catches my eye. It's pitch dark by the time I get set up in the middle of tent city, and I'm dying for a cup of tea. I make my way to the kitchen to boil up a cup, but lo and behold, there's not a single electric appliance in the place. I don't want to start up my stove as it's far too noisy for this late hour, so I give up for the night. Lying in my tent, catching up on my journal, I'm shocked at the language of a Dublin family only metres away.

'Ahh, go away you dopey little bollocks yeh! Ask yer da – he'll help yeh!' says Ma to her cheeky pup.

'Well fuck ye,' says the cheeky pup.

The language is brutal and they don't care who's around. The King of Cursing – the Da – arrives back from the toilet and joins in the conversation. 'Now Carl – if you don't fuck off and stop annoying us with tha' fucking car, I'll just fuck it in the bin!'

This charming discourse continues in like vein until after midnight.

Day 5

The birds are singing at six in the morning, but otherwise there's an odd silence about the place, as if somebody had strangled the Adams Family in the middle of the night. I take full advantage of the tranquillity to nod off again for a few hours.

I'm rudely awoken by a stray football whacking the side of my tent and the shrieks of happy kids, but I'm actually glad of the wake-up call because it's well after nine.

As I refill my water-bottles in the site kitchen, one of those Second-World-War-type Englishmen commences an interrogation. 'So how far will you go today?'

'Not sure really. Clare would be nice, but I'll take it as it comes.'

'That's a bloody long way on a pushbike! Me and my wife walked eight miles along the beach yesterday. You should give it a go before you leave.'

'Sounds lovely, but I'm not into triathlons. Besides, I see more than my fair share of the countryside from the bike.'

He takes this as rejection, and his mood sours. 'Why the hell would you bother cycling around Ireland? What's the bloody point?'

My mention of a United Ireland is met with stony silence, and he retreats to Dunkirk or somewhere. Whether he's got a problem with the subject or is just a pompous English prick, I guess I'll never know.

Heading east, my body feels drained of energy. My get up and go has got up and left. This feeling is inevitable on long cycling trips, and my usual remedy is bananas – something I purchase as soon as I reach Killorglin.

It's a handy-sized town of a few thousand people, and its claim to fame is Puck Fair – one of the oldest festivals in Europe. Held every year on the second weekend of August, the three-day celebration revolves around the crowning of

King Puck, a wild goat from the mountains who doesn't seem to object to being displayed in a small cage raised high in the air. It all goes back to the seventeenth-century when Oliver Cromwell's army swept across Ireland in an orgy of ethnic-cleansing. As the army terrorised the countryside – probably searching for WMDs – a puck broke from his herd and made for Killorglin. The sight of the distressed goat alerted the locals, and they were able to secure the town and protect themselves against the coalition of the killing. And ever since, they've crowned a goat King of Killorglin in honour of its brave ancestor.

It's a busy Sunday morning, and Killorglin Mass-goers fill the supermarket. I stock up on essentials and flick through the trashy Sunday papers that the locals can't seem to get enough of. 'MI5 quiz Gardaí on Islam terror network' and 'Blair insists G8 deal will save millions of Africans' are just two of the many ludicrous stories vying for space with serious articles about what Brad Pitt eats for breakfast and which knickers to wear to turn your man on.

The outskirts of Tralee are shitty enough, but the centre of town has character. It's the day of the big game between Cork and Kerry, and the whole place is a sea of green and yellow. A few brave Corkonians walk the streets, defiantly dressed in the red-and-white jersey of our beloved county.

On the road to Listowel, the radio commentary from the big match in Cork's Páirc Uí Chaoimh is fascinating. The crowd of 32,000 is being treated to a tight, entertaining game. There was only a point in it at halftime, but now – with only a few minutes remaining – Kerry are ahead, and only a goal from Cork can save the day. In the centre of Listowel, I leap off my bike and throw myself into a pub for the dying moments of the game. I'm just in time to witness a heaving crowd of Kerry fans go nuts as the final whistle is blown. Kerry has won the Munster Final. I slither back out the door, and it's not long before car horns are blaring. Honestly, you'd swear they'd won the All-Ireland.

Listowel seems short on attractions. The hometown of the playwright John B. Keane, its other claim to fame dates back to 1888 and the first working monorail system in the world. This bit of guidebook information surprises me; mention monorails and one normally thinks of Tokyo or Seattle.

Train travel is one of my favourite modes of transport. On a train you can walk about, stretch your legs, meet new and interesting people. I've done many long and memorable train journeys across China, Thailand and several other countries, though a train crash in Indonesia dented my confidence somewhat, even though I wasn't injured.

Tarbert is a life-saver. The ferry there enables you to go from Kerry to Clare without setting foot in Limerick. But will I make it in time for the last sailing?

My escape from Listowel is thwarted when a car screeches to a halt in front of me. A shady-looking character jumps out, runs to the boot, opens it and pulls out a gun. Well, it's actually a bottle of beer, but it *could* have been a gun.

'Here! Take this. You deserve it. I know what it feels like. I've done my share of cycle trips, and it's good to be appreciated once in a while.'

I'm anxious to get going again, but his story about a cycling trip he made from Canada to Argentina in the Seventies is well worth the delay.

'Don't drink that now. Drink it when you camp tonight,' he shouts from the car as he pulls away.

His kind gesture gives me a burst of energy, and I hit the road in spots for the last ten miles to Tarbert. Halfway there, I'm astounded to see the same fella waiting for me, only now he's holding a baseball hat. 'Here. Take it. You'll need it for the sun.'

His eyes are red, and he looks like he's been crying. 'Do you smoke?' he asks.

'No. I hate the smell of tobacco.'

'I mean the green stuff.'

'No. Don't touch that either.'

'That's a pity. So you don't want this then?' Opening his hand, he reveals a fistful of weed.

Obviously stoned, he gets very deep for the next few minutes about the art of travelling and the emotions we go through and the lessons we learn about life. I agree with most of what he says, but don't feel quite the same intensity. And then he's gone again.

The cars are coming off the ferry when I arrive at Tarbert. I couldn't have timed it better. A man in a yellow vest ushers me to one side and relieves me of a few euros. 'You're doing it the hard way,' says he. The *Shannon Dolphin* commences the twenty-minute crossing of the Shannon estuary. There's a cold wind blowing up top, but the view is well worth freezing for.

As we near the other side, I get talking to a woman in her seventies or thereabouts. She's from Kerry and is going over to Clare to visit her daughter. I ask her will there ever be a United Ireland. 'For as long as I can remember, there has always been trouble up there. All the people killed and families affected by what really is only a piece of dirt. God knows the country would be better off united, but I don't think I'll ever see it myself. Still and all, I think there'll be a United Ireland sometime.'

I'm first off the boat, and quickly discover a caravan site. The reception is closed, but a friendly Dubliner tells me the owners don't allow tents in the park anymore and that my only option is in Kilkee, ten miles away.

It takes an hour to get there, and I'm astounded by how busy the place is. The streets are packed with people, and more are spilling out of the pubs. My first priority is to find the campsite. Mr Grumpy, the owner, is less than helpful. 'We didn't make any money from your type, so we gave up the camping last year. It's only caravans now.' He suggests a B+B, but thinks they're full up.

I'm annoyed at the fact that this part of County Clare doesn't seem to cater for the budget traveller. It's all B+Bs and fecking hotels. It's as if the country wants to choke you for every last euro you have. Well fuck them! I'm sick of it. I'm living in a rip-off, materialistic country. This new Ireland where you're expected to work six days a week to repay loans you take out to buy shit you don't need to impress people you don't even fucking like is getting on my nerves!

It takes an hour, and I have to stop a hundred times to ask for directions, but finally I find a campsite near Kilkee. It's pitch black by the time I get set-up, and I'm blowing up my mattress when a voice startles me. 'We've got an electric pump if you'd like to use it.'

Gerry comes from Derry city's Bogside – the scene of Bloody Sunday, where the British army gunned down thirteen civilians at a civil rights march in 1972. He's on holidays with his wife Christine, and he invites me over for a glass of wine.

Gerry tells a few funny stories about the Troubles. During a riot in Derry back in the Seventies, a drunk fell out of a pub, stumbled down the street and went down on his hands and knees to light his cigarette off an unexploded petrol bomb. After getting a light from the burning rag, he stumbled off, oblivious to the chaos surrounding him.

The wine flows and it's dawn before I hit the sack.

Day 6
My bloody head is throbbing when I finally wake up. Day off.

Day 7
On the road to Doolin, I stop for a few minutes at the ruins of Doonbeg Castle. It was built for a Daniel O'Brien in the sixteenth century, and taken from him by Tadhg McMahon, who stationed a garrison there. After a long siege, O'Brien regained possession, and hanged the entire garrison face to face. The image of people choking with a rope around their necks whilst witnessing each other's last moments takes a few miles of pedalling to shake off.

The inland route is a narrow country road through a green patchwork of fields to the coastal village of Quilty, famous for its seaweed; it's used as an ingredient in toothpaste, facial creams and even beer. But it's stinky stuff. I catch a whiff of it and nearly gag.

The bay is blue and calm, and I pull in for a break. Looking north, the terrain seems flat, so I expect an easy day's pedalling. Emlagh Point is about a mile away, and beyond that is Hags Head, which, if my calculations are correct, is no more than nine or ten miles from where I'm standing. At the other side of the peninsula lie the Cliffs of Moher, where I'll be in a few hours.

I tuck into a bowl of muesli. Yummy. Even more yummy is the young woman who suddenly materialises in front of me. On either side of her are two blurry objects. I can't quite make them out. I suspect they might be men. I try to speak. Milk dribbles down my chin. I remove the spoon from the back of my throat and somehow emit a high-pitched 'Hello.'

She smiles but says nothing. Then one of the blurry images speaks to me. 'Elooou. Ow are you?'

They're French. I guess all three are in their twenties, and they tell me they're studying engineering in the same school.

They're on a three-week cycling trip. They tell me their names, which go in one ear and out the other. One of the lads has a branch stuck through his handlebars with what looks like a face-cloth clipped to it with clothes pegs. The other lad has snapped a rear gear cable and can't change gears. That means lots of pushing when he encounters hills. He asks if I have a spare, which I don't. 'You might get a cable in Miltown Malbay,' I suggest. 'It's about ten kilometres from here.'

They're heading for the cliffs and then the Aran Islands, and are anxious to get going. 'I'll probably see you tonight on the islands,' I call after them.

My timing is a bit off. If I'd arrived in Miltown Malbay just a few days earlier, I'd have been here for the Willie Clancy Music Festival. Apparently, it's mighty. Pedalling through town, it's like the calm after the storm, and I try to imagine the *craic* I've missed.

During the ten-mile stretch to Lahinch, I tune into the radio in search of news about the Orange march in Ardoyne. Today's the Twelfth of July – there's bound to be trouble. This annual show of supremacy really gets tempers boiling – I know *I* wouldn't put up with it.

Lost in my own thoughts, I suddenly find myself in Lahinch. What a beautiful name – and not a bad-looking place. On the beach, sunworshipers sit and soak up the sun, and today there's plenty to soak up. Then again, there might not be enough to go around – a quick scan of the sunbathers confirms that obesity is now the norm in Irish society.

I really must take my hat off to the local council because the place is spotlessly clean and well kept. With my hat off, I slap on some factor 30. At a supermarket, I buy broccoli and cheese for tonight, and get a made-up breakfast roll at the deli counter. I also locate the source of the obseity epidemic: a queue half a mile long snakes its way up to the ice-cream machine, and '99s are being sold by the dozen.

A breakfast roll has to be the most deliciously satisfying thing in the entire universe. The sausages, black puddings, eggs, bacon, beans – this one even has mushrooms – is sex in a sandwich. If I'm to be executed tomorrow and have one final wish, forget the cigarette, forget the French girl, give me the breakfast roll. Total satisfaction.

It occurs to me that I haven't asked anyone about our historical destiny for a while, so I look around for likely candidates. Two teenage lads exit the shop wearing the yellow Clare jersey with its blue stripe. 'Come here, lads. I want to ask ye a question.'

They answer without hesitation. 'When I'm old enough,' says the first, 'I'm voting Sinn Féin. The others don't give a shite about the North. They only want to sell our country to Shell. They lock up anyone who goes against them.'

His pal is in full agreement. 'We'll have to sort out the South first. Then we'll see about a United Ireland.'

I'm impressed with their political acumen. The mention of Shell is a reference to the Rossport 5 – five ordinary Mayomen locked up for resisting Shell's attempt to do to Ireland what they've done to the Niger Delta. We can expect a few hangings during the next year or two.

Taking the R478 north, I pass a beautiful golf course. This area is overrun with golf courses – in fact, it's known as the 'St Andrews of Ireland'. I stop for a look. People of all ages whack the ball in every direction. A bunch of older men tee-off, not far from the road. A father shows his son the correct way to stand and how to hold the club, while Daddy's business partners look on, embarrassing the poor lad. The son whacks it straight into the rough. Daddy gives the 'Sure, I showed you what to do, you fool!' look to his son, who clearly couldn't give a damn. Daddy, the expert, decides to show him how it's done, and hooks it in the same direction, much to the applause and booing of his mates. Both the ball and the contract are lost.

While all this is going on, a young woman cycling from the direction of Liscannor comes over to speak to me. She's German and in her late teens, maybe early twenties. Her English is fluent – probably better than mine – and she's wearing a red-and-white tea-towel on her head. Yes, you heard me right – a tea-towel. It reminds me of my grandmother's checked tea-towel that was full of holes and with which she wiped every spill, blew every nose and dried every dish. It could be the same one. She's staying in Doolin for a few days and is on a day-trip to Lahinch in search of a cheap supermarket. I note the address of her hostel, and suggest we meet up if I get to Doolin tonight.

'I'd like that,' she says. I wonder if she means it.

Liscannor is a tiny seaside village famous for its flat stones and as the birthplace of the inventor of the submarine, John Philip Holland. He emigrated to the US in 1873, where he perfected his invention with a view to sinking British warships. I think we can safely assume that he'd be for a United Ireland.

A herd of tour-buses glisten in the carpark at the Cliffs of Moher. A lot of construction is going on, and much of the land to my left is closed off. I presume it's the new €22 million visitor centre I've been hearing about, except that it'll probably end up costing €122 million if it's anything like the other over-budget building projects blighting the country. Those brown envelopes take a lot of filling.

I'm astounded by the sheer number of people here. With the preponderance of Yankee accents, it's more like JFK Airport rather than a tiny building on a remote hill in the west of Ireland.

A young woman plays some good Irish music on her tin

whistle, while happy Yanks snap up her latest CD from the stack at her feet. Each is rewarded with an ear-to-ear put-on-for-the-tourist smile.

The trail to the cliffs is mobbed by hawkers flogging CDs and souvenirs. I overhear a posh Englishman complain that it cheapens the place. He's not wrong. I make my way to the thirty-foot-high round tower built in the early nineteenth century by a local landlord, Cornelius O'Brien, apparently to woo his lady friends. Today, the tower is being used to woo tourists for the €1.50 is costs to go inside.

I'm not wooed, and instead join the thousands gawping in awe from the edge of a grassy cliff at this natural wonder. The Cliffs or Moher really are majestic. Reaching heights of over 200 metres, the sheer-faced cliff towers over the Atlantic ocean and stretches for eight kilometres along the coast to Hags Head. It's like standing on the edge of a giant green iceberg. Below, a sea-stack is home to colonies of kittiwakes, shags and puffins, who screech as they glide effortlessly in circles around their little city.

It's a pity to share this special moment with hoards of people, screaming kids and circus acts, but that's life. Many young people go right to the edge, as I do. They pose for photographs or just seem to dare each other to go closer. Each year, they say, four or five people commit suicide here. I stand at the edge looking at the rocks below and try to imagine what drives a person to such a fate. Why would someone jump? Just then, a man in chequered shorts digs me in the ribs and bellows, 'Wow! Isn't it totally awesome, dude!' I think about jumping.

Getting a grip of myself, I retreat a safe distance from the edge, and rest awhile on a wall, where another American strikes up conversation. 'I did a lot of touring myself when I was younger,' he tells me. Turns out we both cycled the west coast of America within months of each other, and we talk about the sights between Seattle and LA. Naturally, he hates Bush – a lot of Americans seem anxious to let you know this – and I wonder what he has to say on the subject of our strife-torn country. 'Oh, what trouble there's been on this green island. Such a beautiful land whose history is so violent and tragic. As the song goes, "Ireland unfree will never be at peace". I would love to see a United Ireland tomorrow, but I think the British ball and chain will be around her delicate ankle for years to come.'

Have I ever heard such sentimental crap in all my life, I think. But an answer is an answer, and I thank him for it.

Standing before a signpost near Doolin, I have a decision to make. The ferry to the islands is to the left and the 'tea-towel' lady's hostel is to the right. It's almost four, so first I'll check if any ferries are going to Inishmore today, and if not I'll stay in the hostel.

At the ferry terminal, a French couple are arguing about something or other. The man behind the counter is smirking, grinding his teeth from side to side, twitching his shoulders, trying to stop himself from breaking into convulsions. He winks at me and says, 'I'll be with you in a moment.' By now, the woman seems infected with rabies. Her face is crimson, and white foam forms at the side of her mouth. Spit lands on her companion's face, and I pull back to avoid crossfire.

Eventually, it's my turn. 'Can I get a ferry to Inishmore tonight?'

'Sorry – the next one isn't until tomorrow. They go once a day, midday, everyday.'

Bollox. Missed it by four hours. Whilst contemplating my next move, I pay a visit to a nearby chip-van. This one also does an interesting line in techno music. It's not commercial stuff either – more like the stuff I listened to when clubbing in Rotterdam years ago. Behind the counter, a young lad with a shaved head is jumping about the place. When he finally notices me, he simply raises his eyebrows, lifts his chin and gives me the 'What can I get you' look without breaking from his gyrations.

'Fish and chips, please,' I shout.

The fish will take a few minutes, so I take the opportunity to check out another ferry operator only metres away. The woman there tells me I can take the five o'clock to Inisheer, stay the night, then take the three o'clock tomorrow from Inisheer to Inishmore. Having paid her €25, I ask if there are telephones on Inisheer. She looks astonished. 'There are 300 people living on the island. Of course there are telephones.' I don't feel as stupid though when she points out what a nice motorbike I have.

Back at the chip-van, my order is ready. 'You disappear,' says the chef.

'Sorry about that. I was just getting a ticket.'

Turns out he's Polish. He tells me how his mate and himself have been manning the chipper for a few weeks and are working their way around Ireland. I'm curious to learn what he thinks of us. He loves it here, but hates the employers. Eastern Europeans, he tells me, are expected to work twice as hard as the Irish and for half the money.

Dinner over, I make my way to the pier. The tiny ferry is being manoeuvred against the jetty wall. 'Beagáinín eile, beagáinín eile,' calls out one of the crew.

We'll never all fit into this, I'm thinking. A couple of uptight Canadians with the unmistakable maple leaf sewn to their backpacks nearly knock me into the ocean in their anxiety to get onboard. Now the boat already looks full.

A crewman takes my ticket. 'Take all the bags off the bike will you, like a good man,' he says.

Balanced over a fifteen-foot drop to the ocean, he raises my bike up to shoulder height and hands it to his colleague on the boat. Jesus Christ, don't drop it, I'm thinking.

The journey doesn't seem like eight miles, but that's what

the guidebooks says. The sea's quite choppy, but I think we'll make it. One of the Canadians pukes over the side.

One thing they're not short of on Inisheer is stone. It's everywhere. The ground is stone, the walls are stone, the buildings are stone. Even the two trap-drivers look stoned. Relaxing over a smoke, they chat away *as Gaelige*.

The pub is busy. I hear a lot of Dutch accents. But it's an American, as usual, who strikes up conversation. Mary's from San Francisco and is travelling around Ireland to find 'her blood', as she puts it. She must be in her seventies, and I'm sure the poor old girl will never see Ireland again once she goes home.

A few old boys are huddled together at the counter, deep in conversation. It's a pleasure to hear Irish spoken in such a natural setting. The Wolfe Tones are blaring out 'A Nation Once Again'. The barman – a young lad in his twenties – is wearing what's fast becoming our national costume: a green-and-white Celtic jersey.

I order a pint. Now, a well-poured pint of Guinness takes time to fill. It's an art in itself. The glass is first half-filled and left by the tap to settle for at least three minutes, and then it's finished off with the final pour. This interval provides an opportunity to visit the loo, boil an egg or just investigate your surroundings. I take the opportunity to study the black-and-white photographs of fishermen and local characters that jostle for space with newspaper clippings, old musical instruments, semi-funny cartoons, foreign currency and postcards from every corner of the planet. A framed newspaper clipping bears the headline: 'The bar that never closes.' I read that gardaí on the mainland suspected the bar was open all night, and a young policeman was sent undercover as a tourist – there are no cops based on the island. Naturally, he caught many of the local lads indulging in after-hour refreshments, but the story simply served to boost tourism.

The three minutes are up, and the pint is served bang on time.

The campsite is close to the white, sandy beach. A few small boats are anchored off-shore. A football team heads towards me. The lads push and pull at each other. I watch to see where they're camped. Experience tells me that these bastards are going to be noisy tonight, especially after a few drinks.

I'm walking towards the showers when a bald-headed man approaches me for a camping fee. I pay him eight euros. 'You'd be better off using the shower on the right because someone has vandalised the other one,' he says, looking at the towel in my hand. 'You'll get about seven or eight minutes for a euro.'

I undress and insert a euro into the shower meter. The digital counter begins to count down from eight minutes, but nothing else happens. I spend a minute of my precious time reading the instructions, and eventually locate a button directly under the shower. I push it and water shoots out at a hundred miles-an-hour. 'Fucking hell,' I roar as it spurts out like a power-hose or an industrial sandblaster. After twenty seconds, it stops. I push the button again and off it goes, getting hotter and hotter. In seconds, it's boiling, scalding, way too hot to stand under. I frantically search for some way to regulate the temperature. Then it stops again. It's bad enough to pay a euro to have your skin sandblasted and scalded, but to have to push a button every twenty seconds is a bit beyond a joke. I've been in some dodgy showers in my time, but never in my life have I come across a method of torture like this. They wouldn't allow this contraption into Abu Ghraib. Then again, maybe that's where it came from.

With a lot of jumping and screaming, I eventually get the job done and leave with a rosy complexion.

'Vive la France.' The French have arrived. They tell me about their day. Similar to mine: Lahinch, the Cliffs of Moher and Doolin. They managed to get a gear cable in Miltown Malbay. I learn their names: Valerie and … no – just can't seem to remember the lads' names.

Valerie goes off to be sandblasted while the lads get organised by pulling everything from their saddlebags and piling it onto a nearby table. They haven't left anything to chance: sleeping bags, sleeping pads, cooking stove, waterproof jackets, gloves, cameras – they have it all.

Feeling peckish, I head back to start dinner, only I'm not sure if I have enough petrol for my cooking stove. It's one I bought in America, and it's the most reliable possession I have. I've used it everywhere from the Amazon to the Arabian Desert, the Australian bush to Tahitian beaches. You can use petrol, diesel, paraffin, meths, whatever's available. The only downside is that it makes a noise like Concorde.

I've been boiling frozen vegetables the last few days, but today I have fresh broccoli from Lahinch. Two packets of noodles, broccoli and grated cheese makes for a sumptuous dinner.

The French lads invite me over, and I sit opposite Valerie. 'How was your shower?' I ask. The lads burst into laughter.

Street lights are few and far between, so the walk to the pub involves many steps in the pitch dark on uneven ground. The Aran wind carries *ceile* music across my path, and I discover a pub hidden between houses. Inside, it's packed, and The Wolfe Tones are still at it. I take a look around for the French but there's no sign of them. I decide to ring my father and wish him a happy birthday, but the noise in the lounge around the phone is too loud, so off I head off to the other pub.

Now this is where it's all happening. A few smokers stand at the door, horsing on their cigarettes in their anxiety to get back inside. There's some mighty music here. An elderly man bends over a bodhrán, a young woman makes magic on uilleann pipes, a young fella scrapes a fiddle and a middle-aged lad belts out a few songs.

While I'm waiting for my pint, a smiling German tugs at my sleeve. 'Hello. We saw you today at the Cliffs of Moher.' We try to talk, but between the loud music, my Cork accent and his basic English, he hasn't a clue what I'm saying. 'Yes!' he says, with a faraway look in his eyes while nodding his head as if he understands.

'I'm an alien from a faraway planet called Who's Your Daddy,' I say.

'Yes,' he says, with an intelligent nod for emphasis.

It's unbearably hot inside. Everyone's sweating. We decide to go outside where it's much cooler and where we might actually hear each other.

Germans are not into small talk. Most of the conversations involve politics, current affairs, travel and different ways to kill George Bush. I like German company. My last two girlfriends were German.

Outside, we can still hear the musicians.

'What is this music called?' he asks.

'Well, I suppose it's what we call Traditional.'

'But this song is in English, so it's not really traditional is it?'

Bit of a clever clogs, this lad. I explain how our own language was suppressed by the Brits. Naturally, he knows all this.

With a stage yawn into my second pint of Guinness, I rub my eyes. 'I'll have to go to bed now,' I say. 'I'm wrecked.'

I'm tucked up in my sleeping bag and fast asleep when the marauding football team arrives back in the small hours. The racket goes on for another hour or two, and then there's silence.

Day 8

I push my bike up a steep hill and leave it just inside the walls of the castle built by the O'Brien family when they owned the island in the 1500s. The rooms are dark and damp, and the smell is musty. For a moment, I imagine myself back in the sixteenth century. I can hear the screams of long-haired wild men, and see their swords and axes. They surround my home, ready to butcher everyone within. I stumble over a discarded Coke bottle, and am transported back to the twenty-first century with a jolt.

The view from here is fantastic. You can see almost all of the island, with its maze of stonewalls. New houses are scattered below, and it's obvious that nobody put any thought into planning. The village looks like the kind of mess a child would leave on a living-room floor after spending the day playing with Lego. Such a shame. The Celtic Tiger has much to answer for.

Less than a mile up the road, a rusty old ship lies on the rocks, leaning to one side. The *Plassy* went aground on the rocks in 1960 – fortunately, there were no casualties. It's familiar to me from the title shots of TV's *Father Ted*.

On the way back to the village, a red tractor goes by with a trailer in tow, into which are crammed twenty or so grey-haired passengers. 'Inis Oirr Guided Tours', proclaims the logo on its side. It reminds me of a small-town Patrick's Day parade.

'Bonjour,' I say to the French. They're sitting on giant sandbags on the jetty waiting for the ferry.

'Are ye all going to Inishmore?' The questioner wears a tweed cap and has a rough look about him. He beckons us to follow him, and we take our place in a fairly small boat.

'It's Galway Bay,' I shout to Valerie as we lean over the rails.

The tiny boat picks up speed, the wind is gusting, and sea-spray gives us a wetting.

Inishmore Tourist Information-stroke-Souvenir Shop is typical of any you'll find in Ireland: a roomful of green-and-white useless crap. I purchase a two-euro map of the island, but fail to locate a campsite. 'Can you tell me where the local campsite is please?' I ask the young girl at the counter.

'Well, there *is* one the island, but it's not an official one, so we can't recommend it. But I'll show you how to get there anyway,' she says, probably for the hundredth time today.

The French are there before me. They're setting up camp, and I pitch my tent beside theirs.

The site has no showers, but has gone to the trouble of creating separate men and women's toilets. One of the men's lavatories is totally smashed. Only half the bowl remains. Every door has broken locks.

There was a time when they knew how to build things properly here. The land was once covered with loose stones, so instead of putting them in heaps, they were used in the construction of boundary walls for the fields. The walls also protect animals and crops from the strong south-westerly winds. The soil here had to be transported from the mainland and fertilised with seaweed. The effort involved must have been something else.

I decide to go for a wander on the bike. I want to see the cliffs and the famous Dún Aonghasa. Perched on the edge of a sheer cliff overlooking the Atlantic Ocean, it's one of the finest prehistoric monuments in western Europe, even though half of it has fallen into the ocean. The owner of the fort was believed to be Aonghus, a chief of the Fir Bolg, who were probably the earliest inhabitants on the island. It's a magical windswept place with a mystical feel to it. I spend hours here and witness a fantastic sunset.

Going back through Kilronan I grab fish and chips, two sausages in batter, a quarter-pounder with cheese and a portion of onion rings from a chipper on the side of the road. I have never before spent twenty-five euros on junk such as this, but my stomach couldn't care less.

At the pub, a group of Germans have linked arms and are jumping to the music, pints of lager in hand, spilling it on themselves and each other. It looks like a cross between a Munich beer festival and *Riverdance*.

As I make my way over to Valerie and the lads, a local grabs Valerie for a dance. He clearly knows what he's at, but poor Valerie is lost.

Just when things are really starting to kick-off, the main lights come on. The bar is closed.

Day 9
'Good morning. I'm collecting camp fees.'

Last night's barman is apparently also running the campsite.

It's after nine and a slight drizzle has set in. My boat to Doolin is leaving at eleven, so I need to get my act together.

The French are up, but nursing hangovers. We exchange e-mail addresses and say our goodbyes.

A small crowd has gathered at the pier. Knowing the drill by now, I have all the bags off the bike and am ready to hand my bike to the crew.

'Hi. We meet again.' I look behind me. It's an American woman I spoke to in the pub last night – Rebecca. She's with her German boyfriend. Rebecca tells me about a cycle trip she did across America. She's sporty and intelligent, and has a comfortable presence that I wish all Americans had.

I wonder if these two have any views on a United Ireland. 'I don't really know enough about the subject, but I would support whatever brings peace,' says Rebecca.

Martin gives some thought to the question before he answers. 'Being German, I think I know what a country is like divided and I know what that country is like unified. Germany was only divided for forty years and that was enough time to make the West German people very different to the East German people, and today, even after unification, they are still very different. Ireland has been divided for many more years than this. If there is unification, will the people even get on? Do they even want it?'

Lisdoonvarna. I was here once before, about twelve years ago, when the music festival was still being held. It's now famous for its Matchmaking Festival, where tourists and locals descend on the town for dancing, drinking, loads of *craic* and maybe a bit of matchmaking. For the rest of the year, very little happens here.

Outside a supermarket, an old farmer looks alarmed. 'Jasus, how the hell do you balance on that yoke?'

He's intrigued about my trip, and I ask him will Ireland ever be united.

'It'll be united by the time you've cycled round the country on that yoke,' he laughs.

In the shop, I search for an ATM. I'm told that there isn't even a bank in town, let alone an ATM. Surprising, I think, given the extent of tourism around here. I have to break my emergency fifty-euro note to pay for my groceries.

Ballyvaughan is busy with lunch-time trade as I cycle in. It's the focal point for visitors to the Burren. This area is a magnet for geologists and hill-walkers from all over the world, and could very well be the place where the Americans filmed the moon landing. In fact, if you pause the footage of Neil Armstrong playing golf, and squint your eyes, you can make out Galway Bay in the background. I decide to rest here for an hour or so. One small stop for Paul, one giant rest for my behind.

At a petrol station, I organise a bowl of muesli. An elderly man walks from the shop, stops and stares. 'You'd want to be careful there. I once knew a man who drowned in a bowl of muesli,' he says, with a sincere look in his eyes. 'He was dragged in by a strong currant!'

'Very good. I like that one,' I say. I would have laughed more if I hadn't heard it on the radio a few days ago.

With Ballyvaughan behind me, I head east along the flat N67 through the villages of Bealaclugga and Burren. Before crossing into County Galway, a herd of cows block the road. There must be at least 300 in the herd, which is massive by Irish standards. The farmer has to hunt them along as they stop and stare at me. They seem fascinated by my orange top.

Cows, by nature, are curious animals. When I went cycling in New Zealand, herds would run beside me inside the ditch, and would have followed me forever if they could. But in Australia, the wild cattle would turn and run for their lives the moment I came along. One day, as I pedalled on a dusty road in the outback, I came upon a massive wild bull. He panicked, and ran for the horizon. He burst through a barbed-wire fence, roaring like a lunatic, ripping up posts and bits of trees, dragging them into the scrub after him.

Cows in Asia, on the other hand, couldn't give a shite about you. They might glance at you, but then they make a big deal of yawning and turning away.

My first village in County Galway is beautiful Kinvara – a tiny seaside village tucked away in the south-eastern corner of Galway Bay. The beautiful stone harbour plays host to a large festival in the month of August called Cruinniu na mBád – The Gathering of the Boats. It celebrates the traditional arrival of turf from Connemara when the village used to be supplied by boat with fuel for the winter.

The tide is out, and I watch a half-crippled man with a white beard scrape away at the bottom of his fishing boat. It rests on the shore, tilted against the pier wall.

A few hundred yards after the village is Dun Guaire Castle, a 500-year-old structure perched on the waterfront. The castle has been restored by Shannon Development to its former seventeenth-century glory. It takes its name from a nearby ancient fort of Guaire, king of Connacht, who died in 662. From May to September, medieval banquets are held in the castle, where anyone with around €40 can join in the fun, which includes storytelling and music.

It's after eight when I arrive in Kilcolgan on the busy inter-section with the N18. I stop at a petrol station to get frozen vegetables and a cup of soup from a machine.

On the road again and in amongst the busy traffic, I feel like I'm back in the rat-race. I pass through pretty Clarinbridge, another coastal village at the edge of Dunbulcaun Bay. Its famous oyster festival in September attracts over 20,000 people from all over the world, who between them wolf down 100,000 oysters. Apparently, there are 700 acres of oyster beds in the bay.

Further on, I approach Galway city and traffic becomes chaotic, but at least I've a wide shoulder to cycle on. It's gone nine and I'm tired after a hectic day during which I've cycled around seventy kilometres. My body wants me to call it a night, so I scan the countryside for a good camping spot. It's hard to find a place where I won't be seen, but a few miles south of the city, on an overgrown section of dual-carriageway, I spot a gate hidden in the undergrowth. It's covered with briars and laced with barbed wire, and clearly hasn't been opened in years. The field is in a similar condition – a total jungle, which suits me fine – and there's not a house in sight. I remove my orange high-visibility vest, as I normally do when hopping over ditches and climbing gates into fields. The bright colour has a habit of attracting angry landowners and bulls.

The stove is troublesome tonight. It keeps going out. I bought some methylated spirits in a petrol station in Clarinbridge, and I'm guessing that's the problem. It takes half an hour to cook up my frozen vegetables and noodles. After eating, I manage to boil just enough water to wash myself.

On the radio, it's announced that Gerry Adams will meet Taoiseach Bertie Ahern in Dublin tomorrow to discuss the long-awaited IRA statement. Settling into my sleeping bag, I drift off to sleep while listening to Mary Harney promise a thousand hospital beds. Or was I dreaming?

I wake up a few times during the night to the sound of lorries thundering past.

Day 10

Friday morning and Galway city is buzzing. It's known as the City of Tribes, after the fourteen merchant families who prospered in the area over 300 years ago, before losing it all to Oliver Cromwell.

The cobbled streets of this university city are alive with buskers and performing artists, and the whole place has an atmosphere like no other.

My mission now is to find disc-brakepads for my bike. Mountain Trail Bike Shop doesn't have the pads I need, and the guy there advises me that I might get them in Dublin – he even writes down the name of the shop. This is the kind of friendliness that Ireland and especially the west is famous for.

I have dinner by the Corrib River, which runs through the heart of the city. A bunch of youngsters are drinking cans of cider and feeding the swans.

Salthill – Ireland's answer to Blackpool – is a seaside resort with lots of cheap-and-nasty amusement arcades along the waterfront. Its promenade stretches for a couple of miles, and attracts joggers, walkers, cyclists, roller-bladers and foul-mouthed families from the east coast.

The cycling here is easy and the roads are flat. Better still, there's not much traffic. A few miles after Spiddle, the scenery gets more dramatic, passing through a succession of tiny Irish-speaking villages with only a couple of houses, a shop and a pub. I've never been north of Galway in my life, so it's like travelling to a new country. I'm excited by this new adventure. As I pedal further west, the remoteness is a welcome change after the mobbed towns I've passed through.

Connemara can be quite bleak but has a magic and mystical feel. It's an open landscape of tiny black lakes dotted around hazel grasses and windswept bogland. It's got hidden beaches with surrounding mountains, and narrow, winding flat roads with the odd sheep or old fella cutting turf. It's a cyclist's paradise.

After Gortmore, I come to Pádraig Pearse's Cottage. Pearse, for those who don't know or have forgotten – or have simply lost interest – was one of the leaders of the Easter Rising. I'd love to ask him his views on a United Ireland right now: 'Pádraig, do you think there'll ever be a United Ireland?'

'Yes. But *I* wouldn't want to live in it.'

Before the Rising, Pearse spent many summer months in this tiny thatched cottage overlooking a beautiful lake near Rosmuc, improving his Irish and writing some of his poetry. The house was burnt during the War of Independence, but has since been lovingly restored. The three rooms have many photographs and memorabilia. I sit on his bed, wondering if he wrote the Proclamation in this very room and what his feelings were as he sat here. The place has a ghostly feel to it.

'Go raibh míle maith agat,' I say to the young man working here as I bend down to avoid hitting my head on the low doorframe. I fill my waterbottles from Pádraig's tap before I leave.

I've cycled for miles without seeing a car. Yellow and purple flowers dot the landscape, and white balls of fluff occasionally float across my path, hitching a ride on the Connemara breeze.

I notice a man in the bog. As I get closer, I can see he's cutting turf. Water leaks into my cycling shoes, and I sink into the spongy grass as I walk towards him. I have my camera with me and intend to take his photograph and to ask him his political views. He's bent over digging turf with a shovel. 'You're working hard.'

'I am,' he replies.

'Come here – do you mind if I take your photograph?'

'Oh God, no! Work away,' he says.

I check my lens. It has a greasy fingerprint on it. I pull a cloth from my pocket to wipe it clean, but as I do so my speedometer flies up into the air and lands in a hole of muddy water. This is my hundred-euro cycle-computer that tells me my speed as I ride along and keeps record of the mileage.

'You can forget about that,' he says. 'That hole might be six feet deep.' I don't bother trying to retrieve it – it'll give a thrill to thirty-third-century archaeologists.

'What's your name?' I ask.

'Peter,' he replies.

'I'm Paul. Nice to meet you.' We shake hands. All we need now is a Mary and we can re-form the band.

Peter is probably in his seventies. 'That must be tough on the old back,' I suggest.

'Ye'ra no. It's not too bad. I've dug this all my life,' he explains, pointing at the turf below him with one hand, and adjusting his cap with the other. 'You know, when I was a young fella I'd climb up that mountain there behind you. You can see five counties from up there!'

It's a decent-sized mountain alright. I check my map later that day and decide it must have been the 354-metre Cnoc

Mordain. 'God almighty, how long would it take you to reach the top?'

'I'd be up there in about an hour, but you'd have to walk up it zigzag. If you went up straight, you'd never do it. 'Twould probably kill you. I wouldn't do it now though!'

'Well, you're a mighty man, Peter.'

'Ah, God gave me a good body so I might as well use it.'

As the conversation progresses, I discover that Peter is extremely religious. I tell him about my mission to find out what the Irish people think about a United Ireland. Once I mention this, his expression turns very serious.

'I'll tell you now, Paul – what those English people did to us, no-one can forgive. The Black and Tans murdered a lot of good people around here. My father, God rest his soul, was a young man at the time and he told us many stories of what they did in our area. There was a neighbour of my father's – a local farmer – a man who did nothing to no-one. The Black and Tans tied him by his legs upside down on the branch of a tree and beat him. In front of his wife and son, they shot him in the head. After that, they shot his son. They carried on like this all over the country. The English stole land that wasn't theirs and tried to murder everyone on it, and they watched them die in famines. 'Tis unforgivable and they've done it all over the world.'

I say goodbye to Peter. He wishes me a safe trip and assures me the Holy Spirit will guide me on my way.

Peter seems a good man. He's how I've always pictured a man of his generation from the west of Ireland, and I'm glad to have met him, even if it did cost me a hundred euros.

Back on solid ground again, I look at my map. I aim to land in Clifden sometime tonight. It's half-past-seven, and I have around twenty miles to go.

Cycling through Connemara gives you time to think. I

wonder what it was like for young people to leave here for England or America without ever having been to Galway city, never mind Dublin. This would be going back fifty years or more. When I first left Ireland ten years ago, I had a good idea of what to expect. I'd seen TV programmes or read guidebooks about the places I was going to. But those country lads might as well have been going to Mars.

Sheep with blue markings sprayed onto their wool lounge in the middle of the road, and some don't even move as I cycle within a few feet of them. Occasionally, white-and-yellow 10–10–20 fertiliser bags filled with turf appear at the side of the road, ready for collection. At the top of a slight hill, I rest on a huge rock at the side of the road, and take in the scenery.

There's a nip in the air now, so I put on my fleece and stop for a cup of tea. As the water boils, I watch the low evening sun shimmer off the lakes below me. I appreciate the solitude. I am the only person in the world.

I get a great photo just before I arrive in Clifden. I'm taking a shot of the River Owenglin with a nice reflection of the houses in the water when, by sheer luck, a beautiful white horse walks right across the viewfinder. Click! What a cracker.

The town looks pretty from here – all the sweet little houses and church – but as I pedal further down the main street, it quickly loses its appeal. My guidebook says 'it has succumbed to sloppy tourism.' I tend to agree. It has a few nice steep streets and pretty shopfronts, and is fairly clean. But something is lacking.

It's almost half-past-nine and I'm absolutely starving. I've not eaten since that sandwich in Kinvarra hours ago. I walk my bike along the street and see a tiny chip-van parked on the corner. It probably serves shite, but I decide to take my chances anyway. It's your typical Irish chip-van with tacky yellow-and-orange menus stuck to the window with sellotape. I get two kebabs, say the Rosary and plonk myself down on the steps of the AIB. The kebabs are surprisingly tasty, and not a maggot in sight.

Friday night in Clifden is kicking off. Young men with short hair – gelled and spiked, twisted in all directions – wear chequered shirts with massive collars, and intoxicate the public with cheap aftershave. Young potbellied girls scantily dressed – their clothes two sizes too small for them – stumble around the streets cursing and swearing.

I decide to head north, out of town. Pedalling along the street, a boy-racer in a souped-up Peugeot speeds past with his hi-fi up full belt. 'Boom, boom, boom, boom, boom …' At the end of the street, an elderly man is getting something from his car boot when the disco passes. He nods his head furiously and shouts to me, 'You should get one of them for your bike.'

I can only laugh. I imagine myself bombing along with a sparkling souped-up pushbike. Shiny alloy spokes, anti-lock brakes, power steering, red-leather saddle, airbag, neon lights inches from the ground, a pair of fluffy dice hanging between my legs and a big 'Fuck off' sound system strapped to the back, blowing the ears of any poor bastard within a mile. Oh, to be young again.

It's drizzling as I begin a nasty little climb out of town. Two teenage lads are thumbing a lift halfway up the hill. As I inch past them, they whistle and cheer me on, running and clapping as if I'm climbing the Pyrenees in the Tour de France. 'You can push me if you like – it's not against the rules,' I shout. All that's missing is my name sprayed in big letters on the road, and the tricolour being waved by an hysterical crowd.

A few miles out the road, a sign points up a little lane: 'Caravan Park 400m'.

It's a will-I-won't-I moment. I'd earlier decided to camp in a field tonight. I have to be disciplined and watch my budget, so I pedal on. Twenty metres later, I stop and look back at the sign. It's after ten. It's pitch dark. It's raining. A hot shower would be nice. These are enough reasons to go back.

No-one greets me, but a note tells me what to do. 'If reception is closed, please find a place to set up your tent.' I do, and within minutes I'm out for the count.

Day 11

The caravan park is well-maintained and has clean, modern facilities. But it has the atmosphere of a graveyard. Everybody here keeps to themselves. They have long faces and hold their heads down when I pass. Not a 'Good morning' or even a smile. Has there been a massacre here that I haven't heard about, or is everybody just back from a night out in Clifden? Or maybe, like me, they're pissed off because there's not a caravan park in the Republic of Ireland that's equipped with a blasted kettle.

For some reason, everybody here is French. 'Devant chateau je le point de personne [or something to that effect],' yer woman at reception says to me.

'Sorry,' says I, somewhat nonplussed, 'but I haven't a clue what you just said.'

'Sorry! I'm speaking French again. It's like the whole of France moved here a few days ago. I'm speaking it all the time now.'

She has a strange accent, and I suspect she's originally from France but has lived here a few decades. She has successfully integrated the Irish 'turty-tree and a turd' into her wonderful way of speaking. She's very friendly and well mannered. I pay her for the night and buy some cheese and a baguette. I fill my waterbottles with brown tap-water before cycling down the road across the border and back into Ireland.

Today I leave the bogs behind me. The massive Twelve Bens dominate the horizon on my right for much of the day. The weather couldn't possibly be better. The roads are mostly flat with lots of downhills. I feel a great sense of freedom today. Life is good.

A couple of hours later, I sit by a magnificent lake and have breakfast with a tiny red-breasted robin. I have my usual mixture of Weetabix and Country Store muesli and a litre of milk I bought back the road. It's all finished off with a cup of tea and some French bread and cheese. The little robin is almost tame. It bobs around a few feet in front of me, begging for food. It loves the oats in Country Store.

I walk along the lake, and as I go, the little bird escorts me along the way, flying a few yards in front and flying again when I reach her. It's one of those David Attenborough moments. There's an old wives' tale in Ireland that if a robin comes close to you, somebody you know has just died and their soul is trying to contact you. I'm not superstitious, but judging by the closeness and persistence of this little robin, everyone I know must be dead. I remind myself to switch on the radio after my walk to find out if an atomic bomb has hit Cork.

'Eleven euro – Jaysus, that's a bit steep isn't it?' I say as I pay the admission fee for Kylemore Abbey. The place is thronged with tourists, but I notice some go no further than the lake, take a few snaps, jump in their cars and speed off to see cheaper parts of Galway.

A fifteen-minute video is repeatedly played in the TV room, and on the way there I help an elderly woman up a couple of steps. I walk by the lake with her for a few minutes. She's over from Dublin on a bit of a break. She's a jolly auld sort with a great spirit about her, but when she starts getting too religious, I have to go.

People leave the TV room as I enter. The film must have just finished, so I sit on the comfortable seats waiting for the next show. There are some beautiful paintings around the room with expensive price tags on them. The Benedictine nuns who run this place have a right money-spinner going on. A few minutes later and the screen is still speckled and hissing. More people stream in. The lights dim. The movie begins.

'Bonjour.'

I've wasted twenty minutes waiting for the French version.

I check out the building without the benefit of the video. It's a Gothic, castle-like structure, and has been home to the nuns since they bought the house in 1920, having fled their convent-cum-school in war-torn Belgium in 1914. They re-established the school here, and have been running a racketeering business ever since.

I turn out of the abbey carpark in the direction of Westport. I pass a pretty young woman on a bike, and give her a wave.

Less than a mile down the road is a narrow bridge with a spectacular postcard view of the abbey and its lake. I stop halfway across it and rest my bike against the low stonewall. There's a tiny grass verge either side of the bridge, and there's just enough room to avoid being knocked down by the murderous tourbus that thunders by. A moment later, the woman I passed a few moments ago pulls up on her bike. 'Some view isn't it?' I say.

'Ya – it's beautiful.' She has an English accent and seems to be of Middle Eastern origin – Jewish, I'd say. I ask her to take my photo. She walks across the road to take the shot. 'Can you take one of me too, please?'

Surprisingly, she doesn't want the abbey in her photo – just her and the rushes.

I sit beside her for a couple of minutes. When she announces that her *boyfriend* would like this place, I interpret it as a kind of defence against me. What she's really saying is, I'm not interested in you – I'm just being nice. Now fuck off.

I continue north along the scenic N59 route. The downhill into Leenane village is breathtaking, and I'm amazed to see a cruise ship anchored in the fjord to my left. The sea edges its way along the deep ravine into Killary harbour and its sleepy village. Mussel farms dot the estuary and an elderly man relieves himself by a ditch.

It's my last chance of a pint in County Galway, so I get a Guinness in Gaynor's Bar and sit outside at a wooden table. My guidebook tells me that *The Field* was filmed here – much of it in this pub. None of it looks familiar to me.

As I savour my lovely drink, a convoy of cyclists pulls in across the road. There are at least thirty of them – American, I'd say – and all look to be in their fifties and sixties. They're dressed in bright clothes, and some have bright-orange flags tied to their bikes. It's a big social event, and aside from a few heavy breathers and those with the John Wayne walk who look like they've been riding elephants bareback for five or six hours, most seem to be enjoying themselves. They're part of a guided bike tour. A van carries their bags and food, and repairs are carried out for them. They and their bikes can also be taken by van up hills and over mountains. Not for me, I think, but what shape will I be in when I'm sixty? Last year, when I cycled 7,000 kilometres across Australia, I met a seventy-one-year-old Spaniard in the desert doing a similar trip to me. I was amazed and hope I'll be half as fit when I'm his age.

After my short break, I hit the road. Within half an hour, I'm in the county of Mayo, a region rumoured to have the highest rainfall in western Europe.

At the end of a grey bridge, I hop off my bike and lean it against the stonewall outside a tiny cottage. In seconds, a black-and-white sheepdog rushes to the small gate, barking viciously, resting her paws on the iron bars, showing off her massive yellow teeth. Two more follow. One jumps up and down repeatedly, while the other – a young pup – runs around in circles thinking it's all a big game. The whole commotion alerts the owner, and a big man emerges from the tiny door of the cottage, waving a hammer. 'Will ye whisht up, will ye! Shush shush. Come here, shush, go to bed, go to bed!'

'They're mighty guard dogs, aren't they?' I say, watching the hammer closely. 'Sorry for causing a panic, but I just stopped here to take a look at that bridge.'

'Oh, that's no problem at all. Sure, 'tis a fine day, isn't it' he says, resting an elbow on one of the pillars.

'It's great, couldn't be better.'

'I suppose you're up here to climb the hill, are ye?' says he, tapping the wall gently with the hammer.

'The hill?'

'Croagh Patrick.'

'Oh no. I'm just cycling around the country. I'm just passing through.'

'You're not a tourist are ye? Where're you from?'

'Cork.'

Willie is a bachelor sheepfarmer in his fifties with an impressive 500-acre farm, though admittedly most of it is bogland. A gentle man for his size, he tells me about the Irish government forcing him to stop digging turf as part of a preservation project, and offering compensation which years later he hasn't received.

I guess Willie has strong views on lots of subjects, so I tell him about my survey.

'Oh, there'll be a United Ireland alright – just give it twenty years.'

He tells me about an ambush against the Black and Tans only a few miles up the road in a place called Carrowkennedy. It was June 1921, and a column of thirty-three men finished off thirteen Tans, while another thirteen surrendered.

A few miles south of Westport, I come across a strange football pitch. It's bang in the middle of a bog, and its rough marshy grass is at least two-foot high and covers the entire playing area. This might explain why Mayo hasn't won an All-Ireland in fifty years.

Further on, a pub beckons me in for a quick pint. As I enter, Kenny Rogers is singing – not a live performance, thank God. Like most pubs in Ireland, it's sectioned off into bar and lounge. The bar is traditionally the male domain, where men drink and talk sport, politics and how Jerry Murphy's wife has gone off with the breadman from the next village. Furniture is basic and the pint is sometimes a few cents cheaper here than in the lounge. The lounge, on the other hand, is more private and traditionally acquainted by couples. Furnishing is much more plush, and here's where the band will play. Here's where you'll also find Jerry Murphy sitting with the wife of the breadman from the next village.

A young woman half-fills my Guinness, and as it settles, she rests her elbows on the counter, puts her face in her hands and resumes her viewing of the television in the lounge. It doesn't matter how rundown a pub is these days, you'll always find a shiny new plasma television hanging between the cobwebs. A pink poster to my left reads how Ray Lynam will play here next Saturday night. Jesus, he's on the road a long time.

At the opposite end of the counter, sitting alone, an elderly man wearing an old brown cardigan rests a shoulder against the wall. The lad sitting one stool up from me is a short, frail man in his fifties, with a massive head of grey hair. He wears a white vest and a pair of pants covered in cement. Beside him, his drinking partner is a much heavier man, a few years younger, and also dressed in working clothes. When he speaks, I learn he's English. 'You know,' he says, 'how you fellas do it I just don't know. The cycling that is. Where did you come from today?'

'Clifden.'

'That's a fair old ride. And where will you stay tonight?'

'I hope to make it to Westport.'

'Oh yea – that's about ten miles. I wouldn't like to be doing it myself now, but I'm sure it's nothing to you.'

The grey-haired fella pipes up: 'Sure, that's nauthing, for fuck sake. I often walked cattle to Westport.'

'Good man,' I say. 'That's a fair old walk.'

The pint is delivered. 'That'll be three-forty, please.'

'That's my girlfriend there, you know,' says the grey fella. She gives a naughty wink.

'You're a lucky man,' I say.

'Oh Christ – sure, I've lots of girlfriends.'

He's not exactly Brad Pitt so I can be forgiven for not believing him.

I notice he's a tiny bit drunk and occasionally leans too far forward on his stool, almost losing balance. Then he'll suddenly jerk backwards.

'What's your name?' I ask.

'Sure, they call me the Bull.'

'Paul. Nice to meet ye.' I shake hands with him, while wondering how many Bulls there are in Ireland.

The Bull is a Wicklow man, married and farming in Mayo after giving eleven years of his life working in Coventry. He's a funny character – always cracking jokes. His claim to fame is singing 'Lay the Blanket on the Ground' with Gloria when he did a bungee jump for charity off a crane in the mid-Nineties. At first, I suspect he may be lying about the bungee jump, but there's a trophy behind the counter to prove it, and as I get to know him, I trust his honest character.

Trevor – the Englishman – has lived in the area for years and is a plumber by trade. We talk about young people in Ireland losing interest in trades like plumbing. 'I was a foreman when I was twenty-one,' he says. He's worked in Africa, and has done over a hundred parachute jumps. I might be wrong, but I suspect he spent time in the British army. At the moment, he's doing renovations in his home, and the Bull is giving him a hand – hence the dirty clothes. Trevor is anxious to get going, but the Bull is quite comfortable and orders another two pints.

'You know, you'll have to stay the night. There's a big sheep-shearing competition here tomorrow. You can't miss it,' says the Bull.

Trevor agrees, and tells me that people come from as far as New Zealand. It's the biggest day of the year in the area – lots of music and *craic*. A must-see.

'It'll start off quiet but by the end of the day, sure any fecking thing could happen,' says the Bull. I picture him langers and dancing half-naked with a barstool around the room.

'Do ye do bed and breakfast here?' I ask the barmaid.

'No we don't. Sorry.'

'But sure, can't he put his tent up in the field outside?' says the Bull.

'I suppose that'd be OK.'

The tent idea is a good one, but I need a shower and a change of clothes, so I decide to stick to my Westport plan, and hitch down tomorrow morning for the sheep shearing.

After a flat, forty-five minute cycle, I arrive in Westport. Cathair na Mairt, its Irish name, means the 'Town of the Market', and it lies by the shores of Clew Bay. Designed in the eighteenth century by the Georgian architect, James Wyatt, it has a neat layout. In 2001, it was named Ireland's tidiest town, and it deserves the award again. The Carrowbeg River runs through it, and is crossed by a couple of beautiful archway stone bridges that connect the parallel streets either side of the river.

Most people come to Westport to climb Croagh Patrick or get drunk in its many pubs. Known to the locals as the Reek or the Holy Mountain, the summit is apparently where St Patrick performed his snake-expulsion act hundreds of years ago. Apart from one or two in the Dáil, Ireland has been free of venomous serpents ever since. On the last Sunday of July, an annual act of penance begins when thousands of pilgrims climb the 765-metre mountain, some doing it barefoot.

Matt Molloy's Bar catches my eye. The owner is a member of The Chieftains. I promise myself to visit it later tonight.

Not here five minutes, and I want to stay a week. My guidebook recommends a hostel near the train station, but I soon learn that it closed some time ago. Luckily, I find a functioning hostel by the river in the centre of town. It's €14 a night. The guy running the place is in his twenties – a local lad I think. He's dressed up for a Saturday night on the town. As I hand him €28 for two nights, I can't help but wonder if he bought his chequered shirt in Clifden.

The television room looks like my grandmother's front-room, and is adorned with photos of former residents performing drunken acts. A tiny old television with broken buttons sits high in the corner on top of a spanking new cable box. A couple of tiny kitchens upstairs are equipped with broken appliances. I like the quirkiness of the place, but the owners haven't done this deliberately to add character or ambience – they're just a bunch of tight arses.

As I'm shown to my room, four beautiful Dutch women rush around half-naked, getting ready to experiment with Westport's nightlife. I try out the little Dutch I learnt while living in Holland, but they're neither impressed nor turned on by my lexicon of Netherlandish curse words.

After a scrub-up and change of clothes, I head for Matt Molloy's. The bar is jointed, and not willing to stand all night, I venture across the road to another, quieter pub. Quiet, that is, until a dozen revellers arrive and take over the joint. I'm not anxious to become part of someone's messy stag night –

besides, I've left my fancy dress at home – so I quickly finish up and leave. Drunks and bouncers now own the streets, so I decide to give up for the night and head back to the hostel.

Day 12
I'm up and in the shower at six-thirty, followed by a cup of tea. I sit outside at the picnic table, worrying about the overcast sky and wondering who the hell owns that massive bra hanging from the line. I've nothing to eat, and the shops won't open for a couple of hours, so I decide to take a walk.

A half-empty pint of flat Guinness sits on a window sill, indicating what day of the week it is. It reminds me of waking up on a couch years ago after a big drinking session with friends, and having a throat like sandpaper. Gasping, I crawl over a few bodies and find a half-full bottle of Heineken that some idiot couldn't finish. I slug it down. Fourteen years later, I can still taste the ashes and cigarette butts.

A man in a yellow vest drags a green hose around the base of the clock, watering some of the thousands of red, yellow, pink and purple flowers that have blossomed all over the place. The first people to invade town are the well-dressed, sombre-looking, Mass-goers. I get a salad roll at a newsagents near the hostel and sit on a black bench overlooking the river, wondering if I should head back to the sheep-shearing contest. For some reason, I imagine that I'll never get out of that place if I return, so I decide to give it a miss.

To be honest, I'm feeling lazy and the lack of sleep isn't making me feel very adventurous. Besides, I've washing to do and a journal to catch up on.

After a noodle-and-veg lunch, I watch the BBC news on the telly. A young girl from Waterford is one of five people killed after a bomb exploded on a minibus in the tourist resort of Kusadasi in Turkey, and another eight people have been killed in a bomb attack in Iraq. We're becoming so used to this carnage that it's hard to properly appreciate the fact that thousands are being slaughtered all over the world for oil and religion.

Outside, I turn my bike upside down and give it the once-over, checking for any loose or damaged parts.

I get a nod from the owner – a grey-haired man in his fifties – who's arrived to see how his son is managing our luxury accommodation. 'Jasus! I hope you watered them, did you?' he says, pointing to the flower boxes on the window sill. I think he's talking to me, but am relieved to see he's addressing his son.

'I did, yea,' says his lad.

Five minutes after Daddy leaves, sonny is out with the watering can.

Day 13

The sky is black and the wind is howling as I leave Westport to its own devices. It won't be fun, but I'm determined to make the sixty-five-kilometre journey to Keel on Achill Island. Anything further will be a bonus.

My route takes me through Newport, a small, picturesque, eighteenth-century town with a beautiful seven-arch viaduct spanning the river. In the late 1700s, a local priest – Father Manus Sweeney – was hanged on the main street for his participation in the 1798 rebellion led by Wolfe Tone and for which more than a thousand French troops landed in Killala Bay. The French–Irish armies made good progress, capturing the towns of Killala, Ballina and Castlebar, but were defeated a few weeks later in Ballinamuck, County Longford by the British General Cornwallis – the man who had surrendered to George Washington in 1781. Sadly, the latest effort to remove the Brits had failed.

Around Newport, I seek views of Clew Bay and its claimed 365 islands, but on such a hazy day I'd see more looking into a pint of Guinness.

Hills or mountains I don't mind, but a headwind is a cyclist's worst nightmare. As I head due west towards Achill Island, a fierce strong westerly tries to blow me backwards. My wide bags are no help – they trap the cold wind, slowing me to a crawl. The rains gets heavy, and my mood turns sour. I'm like a fucking antichrist, actually. But that's the cycling game – your emotions can change in seconds. One minute you're at the bottom of a hill fixing a puncture, cursing and swearing, and five minutes later you're freewheeling down the side of a mountain, singing a song like you're King of the World. But I'm not even King of the Road today, and I nearly lose it altogether when a prick in a Dublin-registered 4x4 splashes a puddle of muddy water over me without even bothering to notice I exist.

At the turn-off to Achill, I leave my bad mood and the busy N59 behind me. This new road welcomes me with a dramatic change of scenery. A misty, Blacksod Bay to my right escorts me all the way to the village of Achill Sound.

I cross the tiny Michael Davitt Bridge and am now officially on Ireland's largest off-shore island, Achill, two-thirds of which is bog. The Irish word *acaill* means eagle. For twenty years, the island was home to Captain Charles Boycott – a strict and much-hated landlord who leased land on the west side of the island. In 1873, he moved to an estate at Lough Mask in Mayo, where his tenants would later rebel and refuse to have anything to do with him. It's from that langer we get the word 'boycott'.

This part of the country is also famous for its 'pirate queen', Gráinne Ni Mháille, a fiery redhead who controlled the waters of Clew Bay during the 1500s, and who was a thorn in the side of the British. Twice widowed, twice imprisoned and condemned to death by Queen Elizabeth, she was eventually pardoned and died peacefully at the age of seventy.

In the village of Achill Sound, I gag on what must surely

rate as the worst pint of stout in the west of Ireland. For diversion, I observe a lanky Dutchman rushing around in a bid to photograph everything in sight. The remains of a dead rabbit on the road becomes his subject for a few minutes, and he takes at least twenty pictures of its torn carcass from every imaginable angle. The lunatic seems quite pleased with himself as he skips off around the corner – probably off to dig up bodies in the local graveyard.

Keel is the main settlement on the island, and sits beside the long horseshoe-shaped sandy beach of Trawmore Strand. I think it'd be particularly spectacular in summer. Oh, I forgot – this is summer!

Then, from nowhere – well, the sky, actually – comes the sun, transforming the landscape. I take a few photos of my own, and head back to Ireland.

Soon, I'm in a condition of supreme well-being and good spirits as my best friend, the westerly wind, pushes me east towards the mainland. I barely have to pedal. All I need now is a sail and I'll be restored to my throne as King of the World. This is what cycling is all about.

The Dutchman is still running around Achill Sound as I pass through the village a second time. I expect he'll get run over by the end of the day.

With clear blue skies and shining sun, I'm rewarded with panoramic seaviews and an horizon that had been shrouded in mist and drizzle only hours ago. Now I can see the islands of Inishbiggle and Annagh etched in the distance.

At about four, I arrive at a picnic area on the N59 inter-section, a few miles north of Mallaranny. I cook up a pot of rice and vegetables with some cheese, and rest on a wooden seat while watching the traffic head north.

A pair of cyclists arrive from the direction of Achill and pull over for a chat. They're English – mother and son, I think. I'd say Mummy is in her sixties and Sonny is twenty years younger. Obviously fashion-conscience, both are dressed in tight, black, lycra shorts, bright-coloured shirts and, of course, shiny glasses. Clearly jaded, they sit down for a breather.

They insist on talking at the same time, and I struggle to take in both conversations at once. He bores me with the history of some cycling trip they did up a mountain in New Zealand, and she thinks I'm interested in a neighbour who recently died. My head turns left, then right, then left again – I nearly pull a muscle.

'We didn't actually go skiing,' he says,' 'because, would you believe it, there was no actual snow on the mountain at the time. How awful!'

'Oh – rum and raisin. Now, that was her favourite, the poor old dear.'

'The hike across Taupo was such a long dreadful slog, but an absolutely exhilarating experience. You must try it sometime. You must!'

'We've been minding her little Puddles ever since – he's a terrier – but he's inclined to shit all over the house. Poor little thing. I'm sure he must miss her terribly.'

I break into a fit of hysterical laughing, and tears stream down my eyes. I really haven't laughed like this in years, and it's clear these two gobshites are a little puzzled. Thankfully, they leave minutes later, and – silly me – I forget to exchange e-mail addresses.

After a cup of tea to calm my nerves, I'm back on the N59 heading north for Bangor Erris. It's recently been resurfaced with those ridiculous chippings that cause bikes to skid at the slightest touch of the brake, and which leave a trail of smashed windscreens. A friend of mine ended up with a broken tooth when a lorry flicked a chipping into her face, so I always cycle these roads with my mouth firmly closed.

For the next few miles, I'm never more than a chipping's throw from the ocean, and high to my right is the summit of

Claggan Mountain and the magnificent Nephin Beg Range. These massive green mountains stretch north, parallel with the coast, for as far as the eye can see. An endless wire-mesh fence, overgrown with wild ferns, separates me from the still waters of Blacksod Bay, and in its own way is a thing of beauty.

'Welcome to Ballycroy'. The sign is cleverly painted onto a large, flat piece of rock embedded in the side of the road. It has a little tricolour painted on it, too.

Ballycroy is in the Owenduff Valley, and its backgarden is one of the largest blanket bogs in Ireland. This 6,000-hectare bog is home to many rare plants, and its winter wildlife includes the visiting Greenland white-fronted geese. *The Ballroom of Romance* was filmed here in the early Eighties, and the village still draws the tourists.

I venture on, and soon I'm in the arsehole of nowhere. I can see for miles in all four directions, and not a house or cow obstruct the view of this windswept, raw wilderness.

It's after six and I'm feeling tired, so I anxiously seek a place to camp. But the landscape is too open, and I can't find shelter from the gusting wind.

After another hour of hard pedalling through the remote wilderness, I arrive in a civilisation known as Bangor Erris. Unlike the cities of antiquity – those cradles of Western civilisation – Bangor Erris is a bit short on panache. Even its public toilets are port-a-loos. But perhaps I'm being unfair to what is, after all, no more than a tiny village with a few shops and pubs. A flick through my guidebook tells me a little more. But not much.

I do a spot of shopping at the supermarket, and retire to a picnic table where a man in his thirties sits with his wife. Not having asked anyone their views on Irish politics so far today, I introduce myself. I get the impression that I've just interrupted a major argument, but they soon settle down and don't seem to mind me talking to them. They're from Belmullet and are passing through after visiting relations in Ballina. I'm not surprised that the woman keeps shtum, but yer man naturally has an opinion: 'I suppose if the IRA releases its statement soon, the unionists can't moan about much else, and the peace process can continue. Then maybe we'll get a United Ireland in a few years.'

It's after eight as I head east for Ballina. For a few miles, the Owenmore River carves its way through a green valley and the tiny road meanders with it. The wind is cold and the sky is overcast, but it all adds to the eerie atmosphere. The area has a fascinating feel to it. I look for a camping spot by the river, but every ideal spot is visible from the road.

I make time for the Bellacorrick Musical Bridge. I remember reading about this strange bridge years ago. I never thought that I'd one day cross it on a bicycle. An inscription says it was designed and built by a William Bald in 1820. The musical bridge derives its name from the fact that tapping the stone slabs produces a different note, and if you throw a stone along it, it'll play a tune. It's also said that to replace a missing stone on the bridge will bring bad luck for life. Actually, I notice a little hole in one of the walls, and feel it my civic duty to replace it. Then I pick up another small stone and toss it along the musical wall of the bridge with as much skill as I can muster, but it seems to be out of tune.

Further on, I come across what must surely be Mayo's first nuclear plant. In fact, this monstrosity is the infamous ESB power plant that closed down a few months ago, much to the pleasure of environmentalists who had campaigned for years against this peat-eating monster that spewed out fuel emissions far greater than EU permitted levels. It might have seemed a good idea when it was built forty years ago, but times have changed and good riddance to it. The next step is to knock it down, but I'm sure many see it as a local landmark.

Further on, I come across a peaceful lake with a dozen or so tall windmills towering above it – the replacement, I suppose, for the old ESB plant. Many consider them eyesores, and birds have a habit of colliding with the sails. But you can't deny their attractiveness, and they seem to add character to a locality. I'd like to camp here, but it's far too open and windy.

A hundred yards up the road, a short hill rises before me, the first I've seen in hours. Just before it, I notice a tiny road to my left which runs parallel to this one. It must have been the old route before they built the N59. Pieces of tarmac have fallen into the bog, and it's no longer suitable for traffic. But it veers left, around the hill and out of sight, and I suspect it might offer a good camping spot.

I push my bike across marshy grass till I'm on the old road. After a bumpy ride, I come across the stone ruin of a farmhouse. Nobody has lived here for at least fifty years, I'm guessing. All that's left is the bare skeleton, of which some has collapsed. The floor is now a bed of long grass, and I contemplate pitching the tent here. But looking up at the unstable gable, almost swaying in the wind, I decide against it.

Around the back, I find suitable shelter from the powerful westerlies, and here I jam my tent between the stonewall and a grassy embankment a few feet beyond the house.

The stove continues to give trouble. It keeps going out for no bloody reason at all, and is getting on my nerves. I can see it being fucked over a ditch sometime soon.

With a hot cup of tea in hand and a few minutes of daylight left, I decide on a brisk walk to investigate the surroundings of my new abode. The view from my front door is really quite unique: out to my left is the nuclear station where Homer works. In front are the Teletubby windmills and Lake Placid, while the building behind me has the haunting look of the Bates Motel. Spooky.

It's a cold night, but my NorthFace jacket protects me from the cutting wind. My path eventually takes me round to the main road, so I decide to turn back. On the return trip, I'm treated to an above-average sunset. As darkness falls, a weird silence sets in. My trusty lamp lights up the way back to the tent. This is a mighty gadget with four LED lights that last over 200 hours on only three AAA batteries. It's not a strong beam, but enough to do the basics. You wouldn't go dazzling rabbits with it.

I just can't seem to be able to get the fecking stove working again, so I end up having a bath with a handful of babywipes. I take a quick leak before retiring, but as I climb back into the tent, I start to get a bad feeling about the wall. Suppose it falls down in the middle of the night. I get out again and give it a slight push – not a scientific test, I admit – but I'm somewhat reassured.

Snug in my sleeping bag, drifting off to sleep, I suddenly wake up again, totally paranoid about the wall crushing me to death. I reassure myself that it's been standing for a hundred years and the odds of it falling tonight are millions to one. About the same as, say, the *Titanic* sinking on, of all things, its maiden voyage.

At about three-thirty in the morning, I hear noises. I take in a deep breath, hold it, clinch my toes and listen. I hear a child giggling.

Fucking hell.

My warm sleeping bag suddenly turns to ice. I'm a bit shaken as I slowly undo the zip. The wind is rocking the tent violently now, and moments later I hear the voice again.

'It's going to fall. It's going to fall,' the child whispers.

Jesus Christ! It must be the radio, I think, and I check it. It's definitely turned off.

'Squash him. Squash him,' she whispers.

I'm a bit of a nervous wreck now. The voice is clear as

crystal, as if she's beside me in the tent. Being the logical person I am, and not believing in ghosts or spiritual stuff, I grab my light, slip it over my head, switch it on and rush out of the tent amidst the giggling to catch my expected prankster. As I exit, the giggling suddenly stops, and when I turn my head towards the stonewall, I see the grey figure of a young child melting around the corner.

A cold shiver runs down my spine.

I look around the corner. There's nothing here, just a stonewall and some grass. The child has vanished into thin air. The wind continues to blow.

I retreat to my tent, and tell myself that the wind, isolation, fear, imagination – possibly a touch of insanity – have played havoc with my mind. But I have trouble listening to myself.

Day 14

When seven finally comes around, I'm knackered from lack of sleep. I leap up and throw everything onto the bike as quickly as I can. Racing for the main road, I look back one last time, and I'm surprised to see the wall still standing.

It's much calmer today and the sun is shining. Luckily, there's still breeze enough to help me on my way. After an easy flat ride in open country, I arrive in the town of Crossmolina, located on the northern shores of Lough Conn. I purchase a couple of breakfast rolls and a litre of orange juice, and settle down by the banks of the River Deel. All manner of rubbish floats by, and I wonder how Crossmolina has let its river become such an eyesore. This area, I gather, is a big draw for anglers and fishermen, so you'd think they'd keep the place clean. Nor am I impressed by the overflowing rubbish bins by my picnic seat.

At Ballina – one of the largest towns in Ireland – they tell me I've missed the annual arts festival by only a couple of days. Though everything has still to be put back in place after a hectic two weeks, I can't help but feel that even in its normal state it's not up to much. Unless, that is, you like fishing, fishing and more fishing.

It's the birthplace of Mary Robinson, our first female president. She's working for the UN now. She's a good sort, I must admit, but – can I be frank? – that cut-glass way of speaking and tight-arsed walk never did it for me.

The town is often frequented by Jack Charlton, that Keano-hating bighead who introduced us to his don't-try-this-at-home system of booting the ball into outer space in the hope it would bounce off the head of opposition defenders to give us the lead. It even worked for a while.

By midday, I'm under pressure on the N59 to Sligo town. I'm in a dreadful mood – probably from a sleepless night – and a toot from a driver's horn fires me up to give him the finger. I normally couldn't give a shite, but today I'm on edge. I recall hearing Lance Armstrong being interviewed about his winning ways. He said it's the anger that makes him so successful. You have to be angry. I gather a lot of his fellow cyclists are angry with him, too, but I don't fancy being sued, so I'll say no more about that.

With no shoulder to cycle on, the road is deadly. The section from Ballina to Sligo is the most treacherous I've encountered on my trip so far. Traffic is much faster here, and the scenery is your typical forty shades of green.

The county emblem for Sligo might as well be the trampoline. Front garden after front garden displays this latest symbol of affluence. The owners know bloody well there's plenty of room out the back, but who'd see it? Not the neighbour, whose trampoline is only half the size.

Anxious to avoid drunken adults bouncing over ditches, I push hard and fast, and a few hours later arrive in Sligo town, a place that inspired William Butler Yeats to write many of his works, and where the great poet is buried. But will Sligo inspire me, I wonder.

Entering the town – some call it a city, but the population is under 20,000 – I'm glad to find some cycle lanes to help me survive my trip. Yeats' name has been adopted by many commercial outfits, from B+Bs to pubs. It's Yeats this, Yeats that. On Stephen's Street in the city centre – let's call it a city, shall we? – a statue of the man himself has been erected. A strange, ghostlike, tall bronze figure perched on a small stone plinth. From a distance, you might suppose it's one of these mad mime artists covered in bronze paint and standing motionless for hours with a view to scaring the shite out of some poor old woman or child. Upon closer inspection, I can see that the torso is a representation of a page of a book with readable verses on it, and his thin legs are long and exaggerated. I like the statue, and I'm sure the man himself would be intrigued by its quirkiness.

I linger for a while on the bridge, under the observation of swans in the Garavogue River. I flick through my guidebook which tells me that the grave of the Noble Prize-winning poet is at Drumcliff, north of the city, and off I go to see where the great man is buried. I'll also take in Rosses Point, where Yeats would sit and await inspiration.

There are quite a few people knocking about on the beach, but I find a quiet spot to sit and observe my surroundings. Rosses Point is a gorgeous peninsula jutting out into the Atlantic.

The afternoon isn't too bad weather-wise, though the wind is up. I can see how Yeats would have garnered inspiration from the surroundings, and decide to try this oul' poetry lark myself. Sure, how hard could it be? Mine is an adaptation – nay, modernisation – of his famous poem, 'The Lake Isle of Innisfree'. I hope he doesn't mind.

The Lake Isle of Innisfree (adaptation by Paul Shannon)
   I will arise and go now, and go to Innisfree
   And a large cabin build there, by Polish underpaid
   Nine bedrooms will I have there, a dive-board and jet-ski
   And live alone in the broadband glade.

   And I shall have no peace there, for peace comes dropping
      slow
   Dropping from the veils of the morning to where a golfball
      lands and spins
   The O-Zone's all a glimmer, and noon a purple glow
   And evening full of the Kentucky fried wings.

   I will arise and go now, for my two-week holiday
   I hear lake water lapping with low sounds by the shore
   While I stand on the M1, or on the gas-pipeline grey
   I hear it in the deep Celtic Tiger's roar.

Heading north, the landscape is dominated by a magnificent monolith; the 525-metre Benbulben is a massive, sheer-faced mountain towering over the village of Drumcliff. This sometimes green, sometimes brown giant – depending on how the sun strikes it – bears an uncanny resemblance to Uluru – Ayers Rock – in Australia.

Opposite a church, I see a sign for Mr Yeats' grave. Children run amok as I rest my bike against the black rails of the churchyard, while crows squawk overhead. The graveyard itself is in the shadow of the mighty Benbulben. The grey headstone is just to the left of the church doors, and only for a solitary woman looking at it, I may never have found it. It's nothing special – very similar, in fact, to the dozens of other headstones around it. His self-penned epitaph reads, 'Cast a cold eye / On life, on death / Horseman, pass by!'

Eh?

A few miles on from Drumcliff, I pause on a bridge and watch a fisherman casting in the river. Beside him, an old lane with grass up the middle runs parallel to the river and disappears into the wild countryside. I give him a wave as I cycle past him and up the lonely lane. A sign says 'Council Property', but the place looks deserted. I hop over a galvanised gate and check out a grassy field by the river for a possible site. The ground is boggy here, and water seeps into my shoes, but further in I discover the field is as dry as a bone. Cattle have been here lately, if the fresh cowpats are anything to go by. Unless the council put them here.

The spot I choose has many fist-sized rocks thrown on the ground, so I pile them up on one side before erecting the tent. I'm happy to have found such a peaceful area, and I spend the next hour wandering along the deserted river. I see another fisherman further downstream, standing in about four feet of water.

Back at camp, I'm on the noodles and frozen veg I bought in Sligo. I've cleaned the filter on the stove, and it's improved, though it's still a bit erratic.

On the radio, I hear a man has been killed in a parked van at the side of the road between Cork and Innishannon, a road I used to cycle myself five days a week when I attended a computer course in Cork city a few months ago. Will this carnage ever be halted?

Day 15
It's an early start today. After a cup of tea and a couple of biscuits, I'm well gone before the council arrives.

My first detour off the N15 is to the beach of Mullaghmore. It draws me for a couple of reasons. It's the area where 1,300 Spanish sailors perished when three ships from the Spanish Armada were wrecked nearby in 1588. And it was in this bay, almost 400 years later – in 1979 – that the IRA assassinated

Lord Mountbatten by blowing up his yacht. Mullaghmore beach is a magnificently curved, wide stretch of sand, and has the pulling power to keep you there all day, but return I must to the N15.

An hour later, I cross into County Leitrim. This comes as a surprise because I didn't think it had a coastline. I stand the bike beside the 'Welcome to Lovely Leitrim' sign and take a photo.

My time in lovely Leitrim is shortlived, as its coastline is only about five kilometres. But before I leave, I stop off in the beautiful seaside town of Tullaghan. Now, this does deserve to be called lovely, not least because of its well-kept two-mile beach.

A short time later, I'm in County Donegal. Three counties before lunch on a pushbike – that's not bad going. The second-largest county in Ireland has always fascinated me, probably because I know so little about the region hidden away up in the north-west of the country.

First stop is at the amusement-ridden town of Bundoran. Families, families and more families. I don't have mine with me, so I feel a bit out of place. A bunch of young lads up ahead are throwing over-ripe tomatoes onto the road, watching the wheels of cars squish them. One is still intact as I pass, and I do the honours by squashing it to rapturous applause, lifting my two legs for effect. I have a feeling I might get one in the back of the head, so I move on quickly.

In the middle of town, I take a left and end up by the shore. It's a rocky, rugged coastline, with bunches of screaming kids scattered everywhere. There are way too many of the menaces here for me, so I forego the amusements and fast-food joints and depart town for a quieter destination.

I stop briefly outside a military base on the outskirts of town to adjust my gears, much to the amusement – though don't ask me why – of a couple of soldiers smoking fags. It occurs to me that these upstanding members of the Defence Forces must have very firm opinions about the border they've spent so much time patrolling. A sergeant – I think he's a sergeant – seems to speak for all: 'I don't give a shit, really. Why do you ask?'

Ballyshannon: Rory Gallagher's birthplace. Scene of the Battle of Ballyshannon – where else could they have held it? – in which Red Hugh O'Donnell defeated Crown forces in 1597. The oldest town in Ireland. It'll soon be the biggest, if its building boom keeps up. Tower cranes fill the sky, and there's a mountain of construction work going on.

Across the footbridge, a powerful waterfall thunders its way down into the Erne estuary. A yellow-jacketed construction workers passes by, probably on lunch-break, and I ask him if he wouldn't mind answering a question.

'Fuck off!' he says, and continues texting.

The Irish name for Ballyshannon is Béal Átha Seanaidh – translated as the 'Ford Entrance of the Hill-slope'. I get a great photo of an elderly woman with a headscarf and walking-stick outside Finn McCool's pub. Cracking signwriting, too, I have to say. In fact, this town oozes character, with some great arts-and-crafts shops, and I'd like to spend more time here. But the world's a big place, so on we go.

It's mid-afternoon when I lean my bike against a wall in the Diamond in Donegal town. The Diamond is a triangular-shaped seating area in the heart of town surrounded by hotels and coffee shops – a great spot to sit and watch the world go by. A narrow obelisk stands in the middle of the Diamond across from the Abbey Hotel. It's dedicated to the Four Masters who in the 1600s wrote the Annals of the Four – one of the earliest histories of the Gaelic people. In 1609, English barbarians ransacked the town and burnt its priceless library of manuscripts, but luckily four monks escaped with their notes, and it's these four men who are honoured by the obelisk.

Donegal town is a hive of activity, with families and tourists walking the streets. I'm taking a full panoramic shot with my handycam when a five-year-old with the mark of the beast insists on kicking at the tripod. My daggered look only makes him worse, and I have to abandon the whole darn shoot. His mother – in her twenties – finally shows up after recovering from her ten-minute memory loss of having had a baby five years earlier. She was probably hiding behind a bush hoping someone would kidnap her mini-Osama and rid her of all her troubles.

'Sorry about that,' she says.

'That's OK,' I lie, 'but what worries me is that he's been here for at least ten minutes with nobody minding him. I was worried he might get run over by a car.'

She seems to know where I'm coming from. 'It's none of your fucking business what I do with my son, you prick.'

After an interesting half-hour, I set my sights on Killybegs, thirty kilometres away. I cross over the River Eske and head west along Killybegs road. As I approach a roundabout, a small, black car slows down beside me and a teenager leans his head out the window. He wants to tell me something, that much is obvious. 'Get off the road, you fucking German bastard.'

I laugh, but as the car speeds up, another passenger in the back spits out the window. The slime lands on my handlebars, and now it's not so funny. The car then takes a right and disappears. I try to forget the incident, but ten minutes later, the bastards pass again, only this time two plastic bottles of water land on the road, one ahead of me and the other under my legs, between the wheels. I'm fit to be tied, and only wish I had a rock to throw at the little feckers. They're only about seventeen or eighteen, but I'd be quite willing to have a go off the three of them. The way I'm feeling right now, I'd probably end up in Mountjoy, but it'd be worth it.

I bypass the village of Mountcharles and pass through Dunkineely, checking every carpark outside pubs and shops for the three stooges. My anger hasn't subsided, and I'm ready for anything.

Dunkineely is a village on the top of a hill. Just a small village, nothing exciting. It's very cold and windy so I put on my fleece. I'm able to freewheel for a good bit, and the view of McSwyne Bay is spectacular. Life is good again.

Life is bad. A few kilometres beyond Killybegs, the little black car approaches from the opposite direction. More abuse, finger gestures, spit. These candidates for Mensa obviously think I'm a foreigner, and I wonder if every stranger on a bike gets this kind of abuse hurled at them around Donegal town. I should hope not. I can't say I've met very nice or even remotely normal people since I entered the county of Donegal. I hope it improves over the next few days or I'll be heading into the Six Counties sooner rather than later.

I'm calm and composed by the time I reach the fishing village of Killybegs. It's a place that's always interested me. I've never been here before, and it's not exactly on the news every night, so I can't explain my eagerness to see it. Perhaps it has something to do with a teacher in school telling us about it being the most important fishing port in Ireland. So finally, after all these years, here I am – in Killybegs – Ceala Beaga – 'The Little Churches'.

Killybegs is a bit of an anti-climax. I've no goosebumps. The hair isn't standing on the back of my neck. Sure, the harbour is full of boats – maybe sixty or seventy, most of them huge trawlers. But the star quality I'd always associated with the little town with the big reputation seems to have evaporated.

Iron bars at the edge of the pier for tying ropes – only a few inches off the ground – are an accident waiting to happen. Though they've been painted mad, glow-in-the-dark orange, I can well imagine someone tripping over them and falling twenty feet into a freezing Donegal Bay. Perhaps in anticipation of just such a scenario, the Irish Coastguard whizzes by in a black-and-orange dinghy.

A man in his thirties is painting one of the trawlers. I don't envy his job. Today isn't too bad, I suppose, but it must be brutal cold here in the wintertime. Rather him than me. He's only a few feet from the jetty, so I go over and get talking. When he's relaxed, I ask him the all-important question.

'Oh yea – we'll have a United Ireland in a few years. It's only going in the right direction with all the peace at the moment. It's bound to happen. The Catholics will eventually outnumber the Protestants, and unification will come about in the next ten years after a referendum.'

One can't come to Killybegs without having fish and chips, so in I go. I order at the counter and sit beside an obese family who seem to be from around here. Judging by the cut of them, fast-food is all that's keeping them alive. They eat like pigs at a trough. Rather than eating one chip at a time, the mother uses her hands as a shovel to force feed herself. The little porkers also have this technique well mastered. It's only when they've finished and go outside to roll in the mud that I finally get to enjoy my dinner and take in the views from the window of a Killybegs chipshop.

I can't relax too much, because it's after seven-thirty. Leaving town, I head east along the quiet R263 towards Glencolumbkille. Somebody many years ago told me that Glencolumbkille was the most beautiful part of Ireland. I guess I'll find out tonight. But with only two hours of sunshine left, and the hilly road ahead of me, I expect I'll not actually see the beauty capital of Ireland till sometime tomorrow morning.

Leaving town, I can't get over the amount of motorbikes

around Killybegs. And not your small little Honda 50s with the white box on the back either, but big, powerful 1100s with blondes on the back. They fly past, frightening the life out of me. One bright spark passes me out on a steep hill, slows in front of me and begins to do a pedalling action with both legs. His impression is good but he loses balance for a second and nearly ends up in a field with a few Donegal sheep. He won't be trying that in a hurry again and please, if there's any God out there, he'll run out of petrol going up the next hill.

It's well after nine now, so I begin my nightly search for a secret location tucked away in the hills of Donegal. I've done a fair bit of climbing today, and the tough going has drained me. The scenery is stunning, but finding a site beyond the view of a house is nearly impossible. Houses seem to be built in every nook and cranny. Have they not heard of planning permission?

After climbing a hill, I pull into a picnic area and boil up a cup of tea. Well, not quite boil, because the blasted stove doesn't last long enough, so it's a luke-warm cup of Lyons tea. I'm not fussed about it really, because the striking views more than make up for my warmish refreshment. Below me, a massive field sweeps down into the sea, and a farmer in a small red tractor is out cutting silage. Or hay. I'm not from a farming background, and I'm unsure what it's called; so for argument's sake, I'll just call it grass.

I remember an episode of *Glenroe* when a Dub moved into the village and immediately went scouting for cannabis. He met Miley Byrne, who was more than willing to sell him 'grass', and of course it was 'good stuff' and he could supply as much of it as he wanted. It was one of these 'towny meets culchie' moments.

Standing on the wall, I take a photograph of the drug-dealer in his red tractor. He passes within metres and gives a smile and a friendly wave. He's probably thinking, Tut tut, look at that poor German bastard on the bike. Maybe I can sell him some grass.

I come onto a Y in the road, and apparently I've arrived in the village of Kilcar, unless the stonewall with the word Kilcar etched into a plastered section has been built here by accident. According to my guidebook, the little village is an important centre for the manufacture of Donegal tweed. Big deal, who cares. Tweed or no tweed, I need to get to sleep.

Left of the Kilcar sign, a middle-aged man walks towards me in the middle of the road with a cup of tea in his hands. I ask if there's a camp-ground in the area.

'Ah no, you'll find no campsite around here – not until Glencolumbkille, anyway. You'll never make that now, of course.'

'Is there any place a fella could camp around here?' My desperation must be obvious. 'A field or something?'

'Camp there,' he says, pointing to the front lawn of the white house beside us.

'There?' I say, a little surprised.

'Yea, camp away there – it's mine.'

I take up his offer at the drop of a hat. I'm a little surprised, but thankful for his kind hospitality.

Tom is a very laid-back sort of man. He asks if I want to go for a pint in the local golf club. I wish I had the energy, but I have to refuse his offer as I'm fecking-well knackered. I'm not sure what his job is, but he's been abroad a lot on business trips. He promises to buy my book if it's published, and if you're reading this now, I guess it must have been.

This meeting with Tom has altered my negative attitude towards the Donegal people. They're not all boy-racers out to kill me with loaded plastic bottles. They don't all eat like pigs. And I'm sure the ones in red tractors aren't *all* drug dealers.

Tom tells me that tourism is down a lot this year. I comment on the amount of Northern-registered cars I've seen on the road and wonder how it could possibly be busier. He tells me that many of the Northerners who flee across the border during the marching season are into caravaning, and with all the drink they bring with them, they really don't put much into the Donegal economy. I see his point. If you stock up your caravan with the cheaper drink and groceries before crossing the border, a couple of weeks in the Republic will cost you next to nothing.

Tom continues taking his cup of tea for a walk as I set up my tent on his massive front lawn. I manage to get enough water boiled for a cup of tea, and I switch on the radio. My relaxing moment is shortlived when I hear about another terror attack in London today, but thankfully it seems that the four explosive devices didn't work properly, and there were no casualties. This chaos in London is just a day in the life of an Iraqi civilian, and lying in my peaceful tent on Tom's lawn, it's hard to imagine so much shit is happening on the other side of those green mountains I see through my zippers.

Day 16

It's probably after seven when I wake up. I'm stiff as a poker and can hardly move in my sleeping bag. I peep out of my tent and the place is silent except for a few birds singing. The grass is covered in dew, and a slug has left a silvery trail over one of my cycling shoes. I fall back asleep again till around half-eight.

In ten minutes, I'm ready to leave. I look at the white house and contemplate whether or not I should ring the doorbell and thank Tom for his hospitality, but it seems so silent that I don't want to wake the people up. My watch reads 8:57 as I take a photograph of the Kilcar sign before commencing my journey deep into Donegal.

My day begins with a climb, and climbing is something

I'll have to get used to, as Donegal is probably the hilliest part of Ireland. When I arrive in Carrick, I'm starving. The small supermarket thankfully stocks my favourite food, the breakfast roll, and I gratefully purchase a couple, together with a two-litre bottle of Lucozade. The friendly lady at the counter is covered in white powder – probably flour – and must have been baking out the back. Either that or she's cutting a big shipment of cocaine. 'Have ye been down to the cliffs yet?' she asks.

'The cliffs?' I'm a bit confused. 'Do you mean the Cliffs of Moher?'

'No, no – Slieve League. The highest cliffs in Europe.'

'Never even heard of them.'

'Oh, ye'll have to see the wee cliffs before ye leave.'

She points to a postcard by the counter, and after studying it, I agree with her that I can't miss these magnificent cliffs now that I'm so close.

'How far are they from here?'

'Only a few miles down that road there.'

I thank her for the advice and decide to postpone my breakfast until I get to the cliffs. I'm a bit worried, though, by all this downhill I'm immediately treated to, because it's going to mean an uphill struggle on the way back. Soon, I arrive at a fabulous picnic area by a rocky river. After checking my map and discovering that the cliffs are much further than 'a few miles down that road', I stop and have my breakfast by the river.

I watch two anglers in the river – they're only forty or fifty feet from me. I'm a bit suspicious about one of them – he has a huge net on a stick and holds it between rocks at a narrow part of the river where any passing fish will surely be caught. I'm not a fisherman, but I imagine this kind of technique is illegal. My suspicions are confirmed when he spots me and immediately switches to his long fishing rod and acts the innocent. I could never really understand the joy of fishing.

Leaving the poachers to their business, I hop back on the bike and head for those cliffs. Each steep climb and every additional mile brings the helpful lady in the shop to mind, but not in a nice way. Eventually, I arrive in the tiny settlement of Teelin, a village of unspoiled beauty close to the cliffs. I follow the sign to Slieve League that takes me up more hills. I pass what looks like a school, with twenty or thirty students hanging around outside. This is a Gaeltacht area, so I presume these youngsters are enrolled in Irish College. A few wolf-whistles put me in a good mood.

More hills after the school, and I finally reach a carpark with tour buses and a port-a-loo. Behind the carpark, a very steep hill leads up to the cliffs, but I'm determined to cycle it. Half-way up, my gears start grinding, so I abandon my bike in the grass, and walk the rest. Up over the hill is a beautiful lake. But no cliffs as of yet. Patience, Paul – patience. The narrow, rough road continues for a few hundred yards, and disappears around the corner. Must – keep – going … must – keep …

I come up behind a small group of tourists – French, I think – and they totally ignore my 'good mornings'. At least the sheep are friendly – one even smiles at me.

When another ten minutes have elapsed, I arrive at the Slieve League cliffs. A Spaniard is arguing with what sounds like a Kerryman about the higher cliffs in Spain. Luckily, they don't push each other over the edge, and instead agree to disagree.

This place is magnificent – breathtaking. I'm so glad I met that woman in the shop, and I take back all those names I called her as I cycled up hill after hill for mile after mile.

A tiny fortification is perched on a hill. It's one of a line of signal towers built around the coast during the Napoleonic Wars, each in view of the next so that signals could be sent to warn of invasion.

I hang around the cliffs for an hour or so, watching the waves below me, and wonder what Napoleon would have been like as ruler of Ireland.

Back in the lovely village of Teelin, an old fella at the side of the road is breastfeeding a shovel. I presume he's employed by the council, so I know he'll have time to discuss politics.

'Of course there'll be a United Ireland,' he says a little angrily, as though it's my fault there's a border. 'But the only one I'm interest in is the one James Connolly died for. A thirty-two county socialist republic. I wouldn't wish this gombeen-infested Free State on anyone – Catholic or Protestant.'

I'm enjoying this conversation when a familiar voice calls out to me. 'How did you sleep last night?' It's Tom, and I thank him for letting me camp on his lawn.

A few minutes up the road, I see a sign outside a beautiful stone house advertising refreshments. I know I haven't exactly been clocking up the miles today, but I might as well stop for a relaxing cup of tea.

The building is a gatehouse built in 1865 by the local landlord, and it's been nicely restored. A few couples sit outside, soaking up the sunshine on timber seats. I'm impressed by the character of the interior. It's got a very homely feel to it, with its flagstone floors, the original fireplace and subtle furnishings. The menu is full of homemade breads and jams. The place is very cramped but that's the way it was back then. I order a cup of tea and listen to a few locals chatting *as Gaelige*. A back-room has been designated the craft-cum-souvenir shop, and I'm delighted to see no tacky leprechauns for sale here. It's all local knitwear and tweed, with some classy looking pottery pieces. But puhlease ... ditch those blasted Guinness souvenirs. They're in every shop in the country.

Old black-and-white photos of locals adorn the walls, and

only for me being skint, I surely would have spent a few euro here. After half an hour in the nineteenth century, I hit the road again.

The road to Glencolumbkille is open bog country with tiny lakes and curious sheep. A farmer passes by in a tiny red Massey Ferguson 35. He turns off the main road and heads down a winding road with grass running up the middle. He doesn't offer to sell me drugs, but does smile and gives a friendly wave.

At the top of a climb, I see Glencolumbkille in the distance. White cotton clouds hang motionless in the blue sky, and a sea-breeze cools me from the hot sun. Below, the village is tucked away in a lush green valley in the heart of wild boggy moorland. A pretty church perched on the side of a hill forms the usual centrepiece, and colourful cottages dot the hillside as the valley sweeps down to a wild beach. The village has been inhabited since 3000 BC, and many Stone Age remains have been found around the area.

Just before my descent into the village, I stop at a stone bridge and take a look beneath. To amuse myself, I hop over slippery boulders in the fast-flowing stream of cold, peat-coloured water. The steel plates at the base of my cycling shoes cause me to come a cropper, and I fall like a sack of spuds into the freezing water, my two legs reaching for the sky. It's only a few inches deep but I'm soaked.

The sun dries me in no time as I freewheel into the valley. It's obvious why this is called the prettiest part of Ireland.

Traditional music drifts from a pub, and I get a haunting premonition that I might possibly spend the day here.

A young girl at the counter pours me a pint. A group of Spanish tourists are huddled around a tiny telly, entranced by the Tour de France. They're shouting for Serrano as he breaks away from Merckx and Vasseur in the final, excruciating climb

94

into Mende after a 180-kilometre day in thirty degrees of heat. It's an exciting finish, and I'm certain Merckx will catch Serrano before the line. As I dose myself with performance-enhancing Guinness, Serrano digs deep and wins the stage.

I try to kick off a conversation with my Spanish neighbours, but once the racing is over, they completely ignore me and bolt for the door, leaving half their drinks behind them. Leaving half a drink behind you is quite common on the Continent, but here in Ireland we call it a mortal sin.

With little happening in the bar, I venture outside. Three old boys are enjoying the heat, and they aren't afraid to ask me what I'm up to, where I'm from, where I'm going, what do I do, how old am I, how much did the bike cost, am I married, who'll win Wimbledon. Eventually, I get an opportunity to ask a question of my own. 'Lads, do you think there'll ever be a United Ireland?'

The youngest of the three obliges to answer, but ends up interrogating the question rather than answering it. 'Ever? Ever is a long time. And what do you mean by "united"?' His ten-minute politician's answer must surely mean he doesn't want a United Ireland – not now at least. He says the occupation is wrong, but that the Catholics in the Six Counties are a different breed from us, and we're better off without them. He mentions trouble with Northerners he's met in the Republic.

By the end of my third pint, the place is losing its appeal, so I decide to make tracks. I have a quick cycle around the tiny village and fill my lungs with fresh sea air from the wild, silver beach before tackling the climb out of this oasis. I stop to take a photo of a couple of Shetland ponies, who oblige by artfully posing for me against a backdrop of patchwork fields, stonewalls and whitewashed cottages. Great shot.

By the look of the road ahead of me, this will be the hardest climb of my trip so far. The narrow unmarked road snakes its way up the steep mountainside, reminding me of the Great Wall of China and the night I spent there alone, in a sleeping bag. Waking up in the morning to rolling green hills and a magnificent view of the giant stone snake slithering over the mountains was one of the greatest experiences in my life. Parts of the wall have been restored for tourists, but this was a dilapidated section with drops of a hundred feet either side. It took hours to climb up to it, and I was the only person around for miles. This part of Donegal has an uncanny resemblance to that open, rolling landscape.

I'm puffed out at this stage, and those three pints I had haven't really helped the situation. The sun is strong, and salty sweat gets into my eyes. When I reach a higher altitude, fog envelops me, and now I can't even see where the climb might end. Eventually, the road levels out, and if I believed in God I would probably be on my knees thanking him right now. I thank myself instead. Visibility is down to a few yards, and I can't appreciate the surrounding countryside. I check my map and see I'm on the summit of a 500-metre mountain. My happiness is shortlived when the lifting fog reveals yet another steep hill ahead. I get a good long run at it, and pedal like a demon to maintain as much speed as possible. But when the road steepens, my blasted gears start slipping, and I very nearly drive my right kneecap into the tarmac. I end up walking to the top.

I'm not celebrating this time in case another hill is hiding around a bend. Soon, though, the road begins to descend, and when the fog finally disappears, a magical valley is revealed below me. Down I go, taking deadly hair-pin bends with the speed and bike-handling skills of a Seán Kelly.

This is the Glen Gesh Pass. I've often heard people waxing lyrical about this place, but no words can do it justice. It's got to be one of the most spectacular sights in Europe, if not the world.

The fast descent is fun, but it's too steep, and I'm suddenly concerned about my brakes. I don't want to die in a rocky field full of sheep shit, so I slow down and negotiate the tight bends with a view to surviving the descent.

At times like this, I'm thankful I'm alive and have a healthy body.

I know I'm back in civilisation again when teenage thrill-seekers whizz past in souped-up tractors towing slurry tankers.

Ardara is your typical one-street town and I call into a typical shop to stock up on what's become my typical diet: bread, cheese, tomatoes and a pack of frozen veg.

Determined to find tap-water, I ask a young lad stocking the shelves if he knows where I can refill my bottles.

'There's a wee church down the road. You'll find a wee tap there.'

'Is it OK for drinking?'

'Oh aye – I drank it many times.'

I thank the young man for his help and cycle down to the church. The tap's a little stiff, but there's fierce power in it, and I'm happy for a free refill.

Speeding drivers are everywhere in this county, and of course the guards are nowhere to be seen. Too busy beating shit out of the McBreatys, I imagine.

On the road to Rossbeg, I follow a sign for a caravan park. It's located near a maze of sand dunes covered in heavy beach-grass, and stretches for miles along the coast.

The friendly owner tells me they're full, but that she'll fit me in somewhere. After a few cheese sandwiches and a hot shower, I put on my fleece and head for the beach. The night is cool, and a cutting wind blows as the waves crash ashore. A full moon hangs low like a huge, round lantern, and casts a silver light over Loughros More Bay.

Day 17

Heavy rain throws itself against my tent. I fall back to sleep, and it's eleven by the time I'm in reception paying for another night.

After midday lunch, I take my notebook, radio and camera, and settle down on a small dune with distant views of what I think is Loughros Point.

The sun occasionally peeps through the clouds, so I'm content. I learn from the radio that a suicide bomber has been shot by police before he can blow up a Tube train. They're saying he's been shot five times in the head. That seems a bit over the top, but when it comes to pulling triggers, the British aren't known for holding back.

Day 18

Leaving Rossbeg, I'm in mighty form, ready for anything. It's as powerful a summer's day as one could hope for – blue skies, blazing sun and a gentle sea-breeze to keep me cool.

Passing the tiny villages of Portnoo, Naran and Maas, I soon find myself heading north on the busier N56 to Lettermacaward. A picnic stop at the bridge over the Gweebarra River is my first stop of the morning, where I boil up a pot of tea. The 600-foot bridge that spans the mighty river must have been some feat of engineering back in the Fifties when it was built. It replaced a bridge that had done the job for more than 150 years. A dozen or so Victorian-style lampposts spread across the bridge look out of place, but it gives it a quirkiness. I'd love to see it lit up when the sun goes down, but not tonight, Josephine, because I've a long road ahead of me.

Crossing the bridge, I pass through Lettermacaward and on up towards Dungloe. The land is very boggy here, and scattered with wild pink flowers. In the middle of one boggy field, five men collect peat and toss it into a trailer attached to a red tractor with a shattered windscreen. It seems like tiring work. A young lad in a Celtic football shirt looks a little overdressed for the occasion.

Traffic has been quiet all day, but there have been many ups and downs, and it's taking its toll. I'm anxious for a break, and my prayers are answered when a few miles before Dungloe, I stop at a quiet mooring by a lake.

A young foxy lad in his late teens is fly-fishing on the lake's edge. 'Any luck?' I ask.

'Ach no! It's been no good all morning,' he says in a delightful Scottish accent.

Ian is on holidays in Donegal with his parents, and is practising for a fishing competition that's on in a few hours. He's well into his fishing, and shows me a box full of flies he's made through the years from fur and pieces of tyre. His family comes to Donegal every year for a two-week break.

I open the litre of milk I bought in Lettermacaward earlier, and have a mixture of Coco Pops and Country Store, much to the amusement of the young Scot. He's fascinated by my adventure, and we talk about everything from fishing in Scotland to bombing in Iraq. He tells me that the shooting in London yesterday turns out to have been a case of mistaken identity – he heard it on the news earlier. Surprise, surprise.

I take a few photos of the lake and continue on into Dungloe. Its streets are lined with colourful flags and the place is thronged with people. The Mary of Dungloe international festival is on at the moment. It's an imitation of the Rose of Tralee – each year a new Mary is chosen as the winner.

There's not much happening around town at the moment, so I buy a bottle of Lucozade and head north-west along the R259 into the Rosses region. This rocky coastal area has over a hundred lakes, and most residents here speak Irish. It's picture-postcard stuff.

Pedalling along the coast, I get a great view of the fishing boats out at sea, and the islands of Inishfree Upper and

Rutland Island. Further beyond them is the massive Aran Island. I know a ferry goes to Aran from the village of Burtonport a few miles up ahead, but I don't think I'll bother with it.

Burtonport is a sleepy fishing village hidden away in Rosses Bay. Dozens of people pack themselves onto the top level of the ferry as it pulls out of the harbour.

Kincaslough village emerges as a rocky waterside landscape scattered with cottages. It has a lonely, cold feeling to it, and being here in midwinter must be awful. Its claim to fame is as the homeplace of the famous crooner heart-throb, Daniel O'Donnell. It's around this time of year that he holds an open day at his house, when his fans can come and have a cup of tea with the wee Daniel.

I could do with some of Daniel's tea and TLC right now. I'm feeling the effects of that Lucozade Sports. I've noticed that every time I drink a bottle of it, my legs seize up. It seems to accelerate the build-up of lactose acids. I'll never again drink that crap.

Two motorcyclists pass by, and the second one raises a hand in a salute. It's the third time in the past few days that they've passed me. They're definitely touring, judging by all the bags hanging from the bike. If I was a gambling man, I'd bet they're German. I travelled through a few Asian countries by motorbike a few years ago, and if I wasn't on my bicycle today, the motorbike would probably be my choice of transport. I'd be lying if I said there weren't moments where I wished I had a motor, but this feeling doesn't last long when I start to freewheel again.

It's twenty-past-four when I have my first pint of the day. The pub I choose is Tábhairne Leo in Meenaleck. It's owned by the parents of Enya. It's quiet enough inside, and sadly no celebrities are knocking about the place, but a half-dozen tourists tuck into tasty-looking meals.

I can see a sign for a caravan park 300 metres up the road,

and contemplate staying the night, but after the pint I think it's best for me to move on.

The evening is overcast with the threat of rain, but thankfully it holds off. Donegal weather is famously unpredictable, and even in summer months it's wise to carry a coat.

After the village of Gweedore, Mount Errigal comes into view. It towers 750 metres above me. It's a fantastic site – it's like a mini Everest – and I'm not surprised to see a bride and groom pose for photographs with the mountain as a backdrop. A couple of bridesmaids wolf-whistle at me, but I can't stop.

I find a nice spot further up the river, and have a cup of tea and cheese sandwiches. I relax and reflect on how bloody good life is.

Back on the road, I keep an eye out for somewhere to camp, but the ground is pretty soggy. A white hatchback passes by with the boot wide open and a couple of construction workers hanging out the back. One of them chucks an opened can of Coke at me.

It's after seven, and I'm anxious to stop. Judging by the map, Dunfanaghy town can only be four or five miles away. It's been a testing day and the poor old legs have had enough. There's a moment of hope when I see an area of woodland at the bottom of a hill, and I figure there's got to be a secluded place for me among the trees. When I get there, it turns out to be not as densely forested as I had hoped. Just around the corner, I spy some old stone buildings with tents on the front lawn. The sign tells me it's Corcreggan Mill Cottage Hostel. I'll check it out.

This is interesting. A stone mill with a massive wheel at its side has been utilised as accommodation. So has a red-and-white railway carriage. I'm impressed by the work put into the creation of this hostel with the unique and offbeat identity.

I ring the bell at reception, and a Polish woman in her early thirties comes out to help me. I sign in and she quickly shows me where everything is. I pick a quiet patch on the lawn to set up my tent. There are two other tents on the lawn – a tiny orange one and a green Hilleberg. Now, anyone who knows their tents knows a Hilleberg. Swedish, of course. High quality and very expensive. Expeditionists and hardcore travellers consider it the best money can buy. It must be a lifesaver here in remotest Donegal.

Just as I finish pegging down my tent, a noisy motorbike arrives on site. It's the couple I've seen waving to me these last few days. Turns out they're not German, unless they're speaking French just to confuse me. They get to work putting up a tent big enough for a wedding reception.

You don't know how happy I am to finally see an electric kettle. The camp kitchen is a tiny building with whitewashed walls and a corrugated roof. A large plywood table fills the room. On it sits a blonde lad in his thirties with a calculator, watch, guidebook and sheets of paper spread out before him. He's poring over graphs and charts, and I know this must be serious. Curiosity gets the better of me and I have to ask him what he's doing. Turns out he's also on a cycle tour of Ireland. He's the owner of the Hilleberg. Like me, he's writing a book about his trip, but his is a slightly more technical work. He's travelling a 4,000-kilometre route around Ireland, calculating the ups and downs cyclists have to endure over the terrain. His high-tech measuring equipment allows him to chart altitude so as to draw up graphs of the hills that cyclists will meet.

It's all a bit scary because we're both touring Ireland by bike, both the same age, and we both had knee operations two years age. I'm relieved to find out that we don't share the same mother. Klaus and myself decide to go for a few pints later on, and check out the Saturday-night *craic* in Dunfanaghy.

It's after ten when we hitchhike the three kilometres into

town. Only the second car to pass stops to pick us up. Like most people in Donegal, the driver delights in going around blind corners at 200 miles-an-hour.

In town, music blares from pubs packed to the gills. A generator from a chip-van spews diesel fumes. A lad with *de rigueur* spikey hair pukes his dinner onto his shoes. Young women totter like deranged ballerinas on high-heels. We really are a cultured people, are we not?

Day 19
Quiet day. Stay where I am. Klaus heads off. Early night. The sound of an elephant roaring in the distance thankfully quietens down after an hour or two. Maybe someone shot it.

Day 20
I'm up and out by seven-thirty. Dungfanaghy is deserted. The workhouse museum on the main street doesn't open until ten. I'd like to see it as I'm sure it's rich in history from the mid-1800s and especially the Famine period. But no time to dawdle, so I get going. The village itself must be one of the very few in the Republic with a fifty–fifty Catholic/Protestant ratio. Riding through the lifeless main street, I wonder have they all killed each other.

In lovely Portnablaghy, a couple of women power-walk with a lively labrador at their side.

I pass through Creeslough and Kilmacrenan on my way to the pretty village of Rathmelton. If I was to rate the towns and villages of Ireland for their feel-good factor, Rathmelton would have to top my list. Something about this place makes me feel strangely happy. A tiny stone bridge leads onto a street lined with colourful houses and shops on one side, and the gorgeous River Leannan on the other. The town is right on the estuary that flows into Lough Swilly. A wide gravel walkway lined with beautiful red and pink roses follows the river, and if you were to cross it, you could wander in the lush green forest.

I pop into a supermarket to buy ingredients for a few sandwiches. Whilst rifling my pockets for cash, I happen across the Lottery ticket I bought a fortnight ago in Skibb. I ask for the winning numbers, and anxiously compare the readout with my ticket. Nothing. Nada. Big fat zero.

Munching my sandwiches on a bench by the river, I wonder what I'd have done with a few million. Would I abandon my tour and go on a spending spree? Would I move to some exotic country? I think I can honestly say that it wouldn't have swayed my devotion to this trip, though it might have made it a little more luxurious.

Leaving town, I swing a right onto the R247 and head north to Rathmullan, where I hope to get a ferry across Lough Swilly to Buncrana. I'm now on the Fanad Peninsula, and glad to see coastal scenery again. But the day becomes overcast and I'm expecting the worst.

The road hugs Lough Swilly all the way into Rathmullan, and for the first time on my trip, the sea is to my right-hand side. I glimpse sporadic views of the Inishowen Peninsula across the water, where I intend sleeping tonight. But I've a bit of work ahead of me before I'll be over there looking over here.

It's not long after midday when I roll into Rathmullan. Delighted with my progress, I feel happy knowing there's a good ten hours of brightness left in the day. Rathmullan rests on the shores of Lough Swilly. It's a sleepy, one-street village with a pier and long sandy beach. As I cycle onto the jetty, the ferry moves off. The timetable promises another one after lunch, which gives me well over an hour to explore the area. I might even chance a pint.

By the pier, a circus is setting up, and there's lots of shouting and hammering going on. I pop into the public toilets, and am relieved to see no monkeys or elephants riding my bike when I come out.

At the other side of the pier is the Rathmullan Heritage Centre, a huge stone fort that I have to check out because I know it's packed with history. I remember hearing in school many moons ago that Rathmullan was the place where the Flight of the Earls commenced. In September 1607, a French ship sailed out of this very harbour en route to Spain. On board were two of the most powerful men in Ireland – men who had tried in vain to end the British occupation. Hugh O'Neill, the Earl of Tyrone, and Rory O'Donnell, the Earl of Tyrconnel, were accompanied by ninety people – family members and followers – all of whom would never again return to their country. This event marked the end of Ireland's ancient Gaelic aristocracy, and was followed by land-grabbing on a monumental scale and the Plantation of Ulster.

A woman is sunning herself outside the main entrance, but when I enter she stands up, follows me inside and suddenly looks all important. She demands the usual few euro we're now expected to pay to experience our own heritage. The ground floor looks like a souvenir shop, and I'm not very impressed. I walk the lawn at the front of the building and down steps leading to the beach. I settle down to admire the view when a worker tells me that the building closes for lunch at one o'clock, and recommends I go back inside. With only twenty minutes left, I take his advice and climb a set of steps to the second floor, where my self-guided tour begins. It consists of a couple of rooms with charts, models and posters about the events leading to the Flight of the Earls. It's very interesting and really informative. There's even a life-size statue of the red-haired man himself. I imagine most of the information here can be found in libraries or on the Net, but actually seeing artefacts from the era and smelling the ancient building is something of an experience. It's a rushed tour, but I'm glad I did it.

Out in the courtyard, I do a quick tour of the port-a-loo.

This also has artefacts and a musty smell, but at least it's free.

I meander down to the pier and wait for the ferry. A friendly woman of around sixty years of age chats to me. She gives me lots of praise for what I'm doing, and I think she'll be only too willing to give her views on a United Ireland. 'Well, if it does happen, I think it'll create many new problems. You'll see the unionist gangs start up a so-called resistance group, and bomb Dublin or some other place. I think the way it is at the moment is nice and neutral, and I hope it stays that way. Better the status quo.'

She also tells me that this is where Wolfe Tone was arrested for his part in the 1798 rebellion. The British claimed he cut his own throat with a penknife before they could hang him. But the jury's still out on that one.

The ferry to Buncrana is a handy-sized vessel. I park my bike up at the front, but one of the lads recommends I move it because when the boat speeds up, it'll splash salty water all over it. Salt-water should definitely be avoided, and I remember a month's tour of Hawaii a few years back when I cycled many of the beautiful beaches whenever the tide was out. Back in San Francisco, I had to replace the wheel rims as they'd been corroded by the salt.

I get grim satisfaction when a couple of self-important pricks in suits step out of a BMW to stand by the rails and get a merciless soaking.

I see the Inishowen Peninsula across the water, and although it looks little different to any other stretch of land, I know that at its tip is Malin Head – the most northerly point in Ireland. I'm looking forward to getting there.

I can't really say I enjoy Buncrana. But there does seem to be a big audience for these kiddie-infested amusement arcades. Golf courses are a big favourite, too, and so is fast-food served on plastic plates.

Pedalling as quickly as I can with my eyes closed, I make

my escape. I follow the R238 and R244 north into the town of Carndonagh. What is it with people living in these parts? Are they competing for some national award for the filthiest part of Ireland? I can't believe the amount of rubbish and used nappies I've seen thrown from cars. It's sickening actually, the dirty bastards.

Carndonagh is the main town on the peninsula, and is basically a commercial centre serving the local farming community. I spend little time here – just enough to do some shopping in Supervalu. Although it's not a very big town, I get lost trying to find the road to Malin Head. But when I see a line of plastic bags, I know I'm back on track.

A few kilometres later, I stop at a picnic area/dumping ground. There's a nice assortment of nappies, teabags and bits of plastic. I try to start up my stove but it's still giving trouble, so finally – after all our years together – I fuck it in the bin. I feel guilty because this reliable little stove has got me through nights in the Borneo jungle, the Egyptian dessert and in the Amazon basin. It's brought me comfort on the beaches of Tahiti, the volcanos of Hawaii, and on the Great Wall of China. It cooked rice for me 500 kilometres from civilisation in the Australian desert, and kept me warm on frozen mountains in New Zealand. Alas, it's time to say our goodbyes. As I pull away from the picnic area, I hear it fall to the ground. Probably pushed out by a stinking nappy, or is it trying to follow me?

Soon, I arrive in the little village of Malin. I certainly have nothing bad to say about this place. It's lovely, and so are the people. They're polite and give me the odd wave. The village has a central green area surrounded by houses and shops, and I admire the little stone bridge just outside the village. No rubbish blowing around either, thankfully. But I'm confused by the two roads going in opposite directions yet both bearing signs claiming to point to Malin Head. I ask a few people on the street, but they're all tourists and don't seem to know. I've come to the conclusion that there are two ways to where I'm going, but I'd rather take the flatter route. I end up in a shop and a woman behind the counter directs me down the wee road to the left. It's flatter and follows the wee coast, she says. A few wee minutes later, I'm on the coast road again. Apart from an unhappy-looking hitchhiker, I don't see anyone for miles.

The narrow road hugs the shores of Trawbreaga Bay. It's after eight now, but there's still some warmth in the sun. A few miles up the road, it turns inland again, and I recognise this place as the arsehole of nowhere. I stop for directions from a young farmer hopping over a fence. A friendly guy.

Further on, I'm amazed to see a chip-van at the side of the road. It's run by a couple of girls no older than fourteen. I buy fish and chips from these Ronald McDonald protégées with the intention of gobbling them up at the most northerly point of Ireland.

Miles later, I arrive at Banba's Crown – the furthermost point on Malin Head – with a packet of cold fish and chips. The road from Malin town has been fairly flat except for the last hundred metres, which involves a steep San Francisco-like climb. Names are written on the tarmac, just as you'd see in the Tour de France. I presume it must have been the finish of some recent bike race, as the chalk looks fresh. Metres from the summit are the words 'Dig Deep', and they motivate me to conquer the climb.

Banba's Crown features a tower built in 1805 to monitor ships. The area also housed one of Marconi's antennae, which connected Europe and America via radio signals. Ugly concrete huts built to withstand an invasion by Hitler or Churchill blight this wonderful area as they blight many a beauty spot on our coast. The spud guns are gone, and nowadays these huts are put to good use by partying teenagers, as the empty beer cans and used condoms testify.

The view is spectacular. Below me, the wild endless ocean crashes against the rugged coastline, and as evening approaches, a beam of white light penetrates the clouds and strikes the grey ocean in an awe-inspiring spectacle of day passing into night. The wind howls and frisky sheep leap among the tiny pink flowers that dot the rocky ground. Or something like that.

Far to my right, down by the water, someone has put a lot of effort into writing the word 'EIRE' with white stones. It must measure hundreds of feet. I believe this also dates back to the Second World War, and was to ensure British and German pilots knew they were over our land.

Two cars arrive and park by the tower behind me. Out of a Volvo steps a middle-aged couple and their teenage son and daughter – a gentleman's family, as we call it. The Kia spews out two lads in their mid-twenties dressed in the red and green of Mayo. The two groups don't know each other. Their arrival together is totally coincidental. The Mayo lads take off in a wild gallop towards the water's edge, like baby calves just released after being housed for the winter. The gentleman's family takes a less athletic approach to exploring Malin Head. They potter about, get an unpleasant surprise in the concrete huts, and take the gravel path leading to the ocean.

As the sun sets, the two young lads are back by their car, sitting on a stonewall watching the sky change. I walk over and we get chatting. The two are driving around the country for a couple of weeks' holiday and, like any Mayo people I've met, are mighty *craic*. One likes the idea of what I'm doing, but the other says it sound too much like hard work. And would they like a United Ireland, I wonder.

'You see over there,' says the first, pointing to the Six Counties – 'that's all occupied land. It'll take a fight, but yes, I think someday we'll get it back.'

His pal thinks otherwise, and the two of them are surprised by each other's answer. 'Jasus, I never thought you were that way of thinking,' says the first again.

'Ah yea, John – sure, I'd love to see it, too. But let's be a bit realistic here – it's never going to happen.'

Soon, the Mayo lads and the happy family leave me all alone on Malin Head. I'm glad of the solitude as I erect my tent by a stonewall overlooking the coastline. I'd love a cup of tea now, and my craving serves as a painful reminder of my poor old stove lying in a bunch of nappies back near Carndonagh.

Me and that stove were together two years ago in a situation not unlike this, when I camped on a beach at the most easterly tip of New Zealand – the first place in the world to witness the beginning of each new day. I was woken by the most powerful storm I'd ever experienced in my life. The rain was like hailstone, and it was as if a hundred men were pulling at my tent. For the rest of the night, I kept a death-grip on the tent poles for fear I'd be blown into the ocean.

The night on Malin is less dramatic. I look out to sea and imagine where I would end up if I took a straight line north. Iceland? Greenland? Maybe the Arctic? I'm only guessing, as I don't have an atlas with me.

I catch the midnight news. The Rossport 5 have been sent back to prison after another day in court. I have to admire these boys and their willingness to stand up to the corporations. I hope they come out winners.

Day 21

I'm both nervous and excited today because I know that in a few hours I'll be in the Six Counties, and it'll be a big turning point in the trip. I'm sure I'll meet a few opponents of a United Ireland – all good-spirited, I hope.

A few miles down the road, I enter one of those deep-deep undercover shops and purchase a yogurt made in a faraway place called Clonakilty. Isn't it amazing, I think, how we both started out from the same little town in west Cork, and travelled endless miles to the other end of the country – the yogurt on a lorry, me on a bike – just to meet in the middle of nowhere. We have so much in common. But I seem to be in no mood for swopping travel tales as I rip its head off and eat its insides. Yummy.

Today's route takes me back in the direction of Carndonagh, and I stop at the picnic area where I ditched the stove. I think I might have been too hasty. I'm amazed and a little disappointed to find that the place has been cleared – not properly, as there's still a fortune of plastic shite up the trees and in the ditches – but my trusty kettle has departed.

In fairness, Malin Head is clean and well kept, but down here around Carndonagh, it's a little inhuman, to say the least. And responsibility does not lie just with tourists, as I've seen plenty of shite thrown from the windows of Donegal-registered cars.

Without stopping in Carndonagh – would you? – I begin the sixteen-kilometre journey to Quigley's Point. It's an easy ride, with flat roads and average scenery that makes me pedal even faster.

Now, I hate to harp on about the rubbish, but it's gone from bad to worse. The amount of shite at the side of the road is unbelievable. For miles, I've had to look at Coke bottles, chocolate wrappers, newspapers, nappies, milk cartons, pieces of sofa, crisp bags and tin cans. I'm sure there's probably a few dead bodies I've missed along the way, too. I can't believe people living in this area allow it to happen. Driving in a car at sixty miles-an-hour, you're not going to see much of this rubbish, but walk or cycle and you can really see the impact it has on the countryside. To amuse myself, I see if I can go thirty feet without passing an item of rubbish. Can't be done, and it's pretty much like this all the way to Quigley's Point. Unbelievable! People of Inishowen, cop yourselves on.

I'm glad to see distant views of Lough Foyle, and I stop for bread and cheese at a petrol station. As I grab a sliced-pan from the shelf, a breadman stocking shelves gives a startled look. 'Jesus, you're making good progress. I saw you in Malin town not so long ago. Unbelievable!'

'I suppose I'm not doing too bad, time-wise, but the roads are easy enough.'

'Whatever – I'd probably drop dead after the first two miles.'

'Come here,' says I, 'what do you think of all the rubbish thrown around the place on Inishowen?'

'Ah, it's disgusting I suppose, but after a while you don't take any notice of it.'

When I'm only eight or nine kilometres from the border, I find a nice quiet stretch of beach to stop for a break. As I sit to contemplate the surrounding rubbish, cheese sandwich in hand, I'm inspired to write a poem about this filthy peninsula. William Wordsworth gives me a hand.

I Wandered Lonely on my Bike
    I wandered lonely on my bike
    Through pot-holes high o'er vales and hills
    When all at once I saw a crowd
    A host of abandoned rubbish bins
    Beside the Foyle, beneath the trees
    Black plastic dancing in the breeze.

Continuous are the cans that shine
A wrapper of a Milky Way
They stretched in never-ending line
Along the margin of a bay
Ten thousand saw I at a glance
Tossed cigarette butts in sprightly dance.

The waves beside them danced, but they
Outdid the dirty nappies in glee
A cyclist could not but be gay
in such a shitty company
I gazed and gazed but little thought
What smell the show to me had brought.

For oft when on my bike I ride
In vacant or in pensive mood
They flash upon that inward eye
Which is the bliss of solitude
And then my heart with pleasure fills
If Inishowen would use her bins.

Crossing the border, the first thing I notice is the shift from kilometres to miles, and how the traffic lights go yellow before they go green, and how the quality of the road drastically improves, and how there's not one piece of rubbish lying about the place. I'm surprised there's no 'Welcome to Northern Ireland' or 'Welcome to Britain' sign, or – as a man in a Dunfanaghy pub suggested – a 'Welcome to the Occupied Territories' sign.

The roads are are smooth as glass, but are narrower, giving everyone less room to manoeuvre. I find myself sandwiched between a high footpath and passing cars. The one thing I have to avoid is my front bags touching the kerb, as that would cause me to wobble and put me under the wheels of a truck. Despite us having far worse roads in the Republic, I felt much safer there.

The last time I crossed the border must have been at least fifteen years ago. I was with my parents when our Datsun was pulled in by British soldiers. They were youngsters really, and didn't call us Fenian bastards – contrary to what I'd been led to expect. The speed ramps, checkpoints and soldiers made it seem like a war zone, which I suppose it was. I've since had much worse experiences with militaries, such as being quizzed by Chinese soldiers, and being arrested and interrogated by the Indonesian army after they shot dead fourteen students at a Jakarta demonstration in 1998. They'd seen me filming it, and I was held for two hours on suspicion of being a foreign journalist without a permit. A CNN cameraman was shot dead on the same night. I was lucky to get my camera back, and even luckier not to have been killed during the chaos.

Nationalists call it Derry. Unionists call it Londonderry, and others who don't want to offend simply call it Stroke City. It derives its name from the Irish Doire Calgach, meaning 'The Oak Grove of Calgach'. Locals also know it as the Maiden City, as it's never been conquered, or so they say.

Arriving at the edge of Derry city, I honestly haven't a clue where I'm going, and I hope to spot a tourist-information sign soon. That's another plus about the North – the signs are impeccable, and there's no chance of getting lost, and – who knows – battered.

With the change of currency, I stop at the first ATM I see, and stock up on some sterling. After a couple of hairy round-abouts, I find myself heading south along the Foyle embankment that runs with the Foyle River. Across the road I see some luxury coaches parked outside the tourist office or – ex*cuuuse* me! – Derry Visitor and Convention Bureau. Inside, it's more like a library than a tourist office. It's well laid out and stacked with hundreds of leaflets and brochures concerning Derry, Northern Ireland and – surprisingly – a wealth of information about the Republic and even Cork. It's crammed with backpacking Australians, noisy Americans, a couple of German women and a few lost-looking Chinese.

I spend a half-hour flicking through pamphlets and reading the local history, and I learn a little about the city I've just arrived in. It goes back to the sixth century, when it developed around a monastery. Since being built in the early 1600s, the walls encircling the old city have withstood many sieges – the longest being 105 days – and have never been breached. In the nineteenth century, it was one of the main ports for migration to America. They say it played a vital role in the trade of linen shirts, and I'm a little shocked to read that, to this day, Derry still supplies the US president with twelve free shirts every year.

The city, of course, was at the centre of the Troubles in the Sixties and Seventies. The two areas that interest me most are the Bogside – predominantly Catholic – and the Waterside, predominantly Protestant. They're at opposite ends of the River Foyle, as well as being poles apart on the political spectrum. I'm expecting no surprises to the answers I'll get from each area, but I intend to ask five people from both sides their views on you-know-what.

I cycle through the Shipquay Gate entrance of the old city walls, and I'm stunned at their thickness – nine metres. No wonder they were never breached.

The town is bustling with activity, as the locals rush around with bursting shopping bags. One man, I notice, walks quickly and in a trance, clutching a shiny new box against his chest. He's hurrying home to try out the latest DVD player.

There's a great atmosphere about the place, and I sense a fierce community spirit, with people constantly stopping to talk with one another. I would have expected the opposite in such a divided city.

115

A short cycle down Butcher's Street and through Butcher's Gate reveals a tricolour, and something tells me I must be in the Bogside. Looking back at the grey city walls, white graffiti stands out a mile: 'REAL IRA'; 'PSNI OUT'; 'SDLP OUT'. I wonder if this reflects the general view of the people in the area. I'm about to find out.

Powerful murals on the gable ends of houses along Rossville Street depict the sad and violent history of the area. The first I see is the famous black-and-white image of a young boy wearing a gas mask and holding a petrol bomb. Another is of a British soldier breaking down a door with a sledgehammer. These events occurred here in the Seventies but could just as well be a depiction of today's happenings in Basra. More murals commemorate Bloody Sunday and the Battle of the Bogside, and the sheer quality of the artwork seems to make them come alive.

I'm standing at the intersection of Fahan and Rossville Streets, beside one of the most famous political landmarks in the world: Free Derry Corner. 'You Are Now Entering Free Derry' is written in two-foot-high letters on a white wall – originally the gable of a house on Lecky Road. This area was at the heart of the civil rights marches in the late Sixties. It's been a symbol of resistance ever since, and it's eerie to be standing beside something that growing up I'd seen so many times on television and in newspapers.

A few yards further up the street is the Hunger Striker's Memorial. The *H*-shaped monument contains the names of some of the volunteers who died during the Troubles. As I stare at the names of Bobby Sands and his comrades, a middle-aged couple and a young boy come across the road to view the memorial.

It's a small world, is it not? Immediately recognising my west Cork accent, Noel tells me he's from Bantry, and is travelling with his wife and, if I heard right, their teenage grandson. Noel and his wife are a placid, friendly couple, and the young lad is well behaved. Noel thinks there *will* be a United Ireland, but that he'll never see it in his lifetime. His wife is of similar opinion, and tells me how badly the Catholics were treated in Enniskillen, where she grew up. The grandson, who has an English accent, is adamant that it will never happen, saying that the two sides will never ever get on. Wise words from a young mind, but I hope he's wrong.

Ten minutes later, I meet the family again at the Bloody Sunday Memorial. This simple obelisk commemorates the civilians shot dead by the British army on 30 January 1972. I scan the names of those innocent people murdered seven months before I was born. Looking around at the simple terrace houses, one cannot but admire this community for what it's endured.

Noel, his wife and their grandson have qualified as my first three interviewees, so I go walkabout in the Bogside for two more people to quiz. I push my bike along the footpath of a side street and come across a hunched woman standing in her own front door and smoking a cigarette. She's very stand-offish as I introduce myself. I can't blame her. Once she finds out my mission, she relaxes. 'Well, of course all of us here would love to see it happen. Yes, I think it'll happen in the next five to ten years. It's never been so close. There's been enough repression, and God knows we've gone through a lot of it in the last thirty years. I hope it all achieves something.' She warns me to be careful where I put my question.

Further west, in another estate, I pass three young lads walking in the middle of the road. Two are dressed in Celtic jerseys, the third in the red and white of Derry City FC. They have a ball and are heading off for a kickabout. 'Nice bike,' one says to me. I stop to talk, and it seems they're fascinated by the bike and where I'm sleeping and all the other usual questions. 'So come here', says I, 'is there going to be a United Ireland?'

The two in Celtic shirts look troubled by the question, but their pal is more copped on: 'Tiocfaidh ar la!' he says – Our day will come – and the other two give a quick shout in agreement. But they're much more interested in how many punctures I've had.

They give me a push as I head off back towards the Foyle River.

Happy to have gotten five answers, my next stop is the Waterside. I cross over the blue Craigavon Bridge into Duke Street. The bridge is apparently the only double-decker road bridge in Europe.

I know there are murals in the area, but I haven't a clue where to find them, and there's no mention on the map. I pull over beside an elderly man leaning against a wall outside a pub to ask for directions. 'What the hell do you want to see them for?' he asks, bewildered and not pleased.

'Well, I'm just doing the tourist thing, I suppose, and might as well see them as I'm here.'

He scratches his fuzzy head of hair. 'OK. You need to get to Bond Street. Now, let me think – go up this street here and turn right at the second roundabout, then I think it's your second left. You can see all the bloody murals you want then.'

He's a little gruff but otherwise friendly enough, and I sense that he won't react badly if I broach the thorny subject of a United Ireland. 'I honestly couldn't care less,' he says, to my utter amazement. 'Whether I'm governed by the Brits or the Paddies, I'll still have to work and pay my taxes. The whole thing's a load of bollocks, to be honest.'

I pedal on through the first roundabout, wondering if people like him are not so far off the mark.

There's no mistaking Bond Street. Red, white and blue has been splashed on every paintable surface. Shocking murals glorifying the right-wing UDA and UFF paramilitaries share walls with signs advertising coal and oil. A disturbing mural depicts a battle scene featuring an evil-looking skeleton in a British uniform with a UFF badge on its sleeve grasping a tattered Union Jack and blood-spattered sword. He charges forward after killing what looks like an Irish soldier, whose body lies on the ground with a broken flag-pole protruding from his stomach. The backdrop to the battle is Free Derry Corner, and the image seems to depict a massacre in the Bogside. From where I'm standing, it all seems a bit fascist. A quote from the mural reads, 'We determine the guilty, we decide the punishment'. DIY jurisprudence, I think it's called.

A nervousness sets in, and I wonder if it's safe even to be here, let alone goad the locals by raising such a delicate subject as a ... well, you know what.

But I haven't cycled halfway round the country to give up now. I'm including the man I met ten minutes ago on Duke Street, so I've four people left to ask. This street is mostly lined with town houses, so there's not too many people around, but way down at the end, I spot a couple pushing a pram and cycle down towards them. I introduce myself and get the 'Who's the weirdo' look. I can't say they're overjoyed to see me, yet both are prepared to talk.

'No!' he says, with a are-you-trying-to-annoy-me look. 'There'll never be a so-called United Ireland. Maybe united with Britain – now that *would* be a good thing. We've been here hundreds of years and have as much right to be here as the next person. We're the people who made the North the way it is. That lot might not call themselves British, but they should thank the queen and our government for the good roads and good benefits we have up here. This fella here, he'll always be British. We're never going to give all that away.'

His wife is a bit of an echo chamber. 'No! We're far better off here. We don't pay for school books and have free medical treatment and stuff like that. It's a much better life, and even the Catholics wouldn't be stupid enough to throw that away.'

Further on, I ask an elderly man walking his dog. 'I've just two words for you my friend: No Surrender. Now on your bike.' That's six words, but who's counting? Beside, he says this with an infectious laugh, and it even brings a smile to my face.

Beginning to relax and for some reason confident that nobody's going to kill me, I approach a fella festooned with tattoos: Rangers, UDA, Mum, Samantha (though it looks as though he's made an effort to scratch out Samantha). The most accurate description of this lad would be 'hard fucker'. 'Believe you me – the Freestaters are much better off without our problems,' he says. Now that's what I call a thoughtful reply.

Having filled my quota and still in possession of ten fingers, ten toes, I leave the Waterside. I'm lucky – in more ways than one – to find myself on the Limavady Road, and away from Derry. It's gone six, and I'm cycling north-east along the A2. Not much scenery to be seen here, though an Arab would probably describe it as heaven on earth. Studying the map, I notice a wooded area in Ballykelly a couple of hours up the road. This should make a good camping site.

With a flat ride, I arrive at the woods at eight. A few cars are parked in the carpark, but otherwise the place is quiet and fairly deserted. According to an information board, it was the first state forest. It's dense with mature trees, and should be easy to hide a tent in. My plan is to wait until everybody goes home, and then I'll seek a good spot.

I sit down at a picnic table, listening to my radio while stuffing myself with anything edible. I know Ballykelly is only down the road, so I'll stock up in the morning. The midges are wicked here, and the little feckers have taken a keen interest in me.

When the coast is clear, I push my bike through the forest and up an old service track that hasn't been used for years.

There's no obvious place to pitch my tent, so I end up clearing an area of dead branches and pine needles. After discovering an old stump among the dead branches, I have to look for another spot. I'm deep inside the forest now, but it could as easily be classed as jungle. I eventually find a perfect spot in a clearing, and make it home for the night. As I settle into the sleeping bag, I hear a dog barking in the distance. It can only be a hundred yards away, and I can't say I'm happy to hear it. I turn off my radio as not to draw attention. I'm surprised there's anyone out in the woods so late. Now I can hear low voices. I estimate two, maybe three men. They seem to be walking towards my tent. I'm suddenly reminded of camping in the Amazon and Borneo, only there I felt safe. The voices stop. The men turn. They head away. I let out a little whimper of relief.

Day 22

The sun peeps through the trees as I drag my bike down the hill again, just after eight. My tent is soaked with condensation so I lay it out in the carpark to dry. After the carry-on last night, I'm looking forward to moving on. I'm not that hungry as I pass the tiny village of Ballykelly, so I decide to have breakfast in Limavady.

A couple of hours later, after crossing the River Roe, I find myself on Main Street, Limavady. It's been a flat ride all the way, with little to write home about. It's a town with a friendly feel to it, and is well planned. I find a bike shop on Catherine Street but, alas, they don't have my brand of disc-brake. I buy a couple of spare tubes.

At an ATM, I withdraw £100. Just as I'm about to jump on my bike again, a man approaches me. 'Well now, where have you cycled from?'

He's a cleric of some sort – a broad fella in his late sixties, I'd say. I tell him what I'm up to and he tells me something about himself. He's a Presbyterian chaplin who works in a local hospital. He doesn't mind telling me his name – William – so I don't mind telling him mine. Though he's naturally against a United Ireland, he's anxious to impress on me that his opposition is complex, and that it would take a long time to explain it. He suggests we discuss it over a coffee in town, where we can talk in more depth.

William knows everybody in town, wishing them good morning and cracking jokes with them as I push my bike beside him. 'See this fella here – imagine he's cycled all the ways from Cork. Do you not think he's mad?'

Concerned about me leaving my bike on the street, he asks workers he knows at a petrol station if I can leave it out the back. I'm impressed at how outgoing this William is, and I can't ever remember meeting anyone with such a community spirit. He's in town to have his spectacles repaired, and insists he gets it done before our coffee. It'll only take a few minutes, he says.

The jewellers is on the main street, so we haven't far to go, but William's celebrity-like status makes the journey twice as long as it should. I'm not complaining, as I find the whole thing very intriguing. I'm learning quite a lot about the Northern people and their way of life.

'See that house there? The lady that lived there wrote the beautiful song "The Londonderry Air".'

This tune is more famously known as 'Danny Boy'.

Outside a solicitor's office, we bump into William's friend, Richard. A man in his fifties, he's dressed in a shirt and tie. 'Now Paul, ask Richard your question while I get my glasses fixed, and by the time I'm finished, Richard will have your question answered. I'm sure he'll have a very good answer for you.'

Richard comes across as having an honest and realistic nature, which I guess is reflected in his answer. 'Well Paul, "ever" is a long time, I suppose, but I don't think it will ever happen. People on either side of the divide are getting more extremist, which is dangerous. My own business has been burnt twice by the Provos over the years. Attacked with petrol bombs. Nationalists have had their share of abuse, too. In Limavady, both sides are getting on better now than ever, especially the older generations. We're sick of it all really. God only knows what the future holds, but a United Ireland, I don't think so. But again, "ever" is a long time.'

He tells me he was an active member of the Unionist Party in his younger days, and supports things like an All-Ireland rugby team and is a strong supporter of the Northern Ireland soccer team.

William surfaces only minutes later. 'Well, Richard – did you hear Mr Blair saying how the IRA were good little boys compared to London bombers?'

After a good laugh, they part company, and William takes me down the pedestrianised Market Street to a coffee shop. I record out conversation with my dictaphone, which, when I listen to it later, turns out to prefer the noise of stacking plates, children crying and everyone else's voice but William's. Being a Presbyterian, his perspective is not unnaturally unionist, yet he will on occasion offer some criticism of the loyalist community. We spend an hour discussing everything, including Home Rule, the support the supposedly neutral Republic gave to Britain in the Second World War, the preservation of the Irish language in the North, and the Orange marches. William is opposed to the Orange parades, especially the 'hangers on' who, he says, terrorise his Roman Catholic neighbours.

We leave the café and he points me in the direction of Coleraine. He recommends the A2 – it goes right around the coast to Belfast. But just outside Limavady, I see a signpost with a bicycle symbol. Route 93 seems to be a narrow country road leading up a mountain, and I'm thinking that the top will surely provide views of Limavady and Lough Foyle.

Up I go, and after a couple of miles it becomes more of a mountaineering expedition, with very steep climbs that involve a lot of pushing. My rear brakes have been screeching since I left town, and when I can't stick it any longer, I stop to turn the bike upside down, much to the amusement of the cattle in the field. With the bags and the back wheel off, I can't seem to find the problem, so I swap the worn discs with the spare ones. Suddenly, a helicopter appears and circles above. It continues for a few minutes, getting closer and closer, and then just as suddenly departs. I don't know if it was an army one or what, but they were very curious to know what I was up to. With my bike fixed and my bomb planted, I continue up the hill.

Judging by my torn and battered map, the hill I'm on is the 384-metre Binevenagh. My half-hour climb is well rewarded though, with spectacular views of the triangular Magilligan Point – home to an army firing range – and distant Portstewart. It's virtually a treeless landscape, with open green fields. There's a fair wind up here, but it's a perfect summer's day and traffic is non-existent.

After a tiring few hours, the descent begins. My brakes are totally shagged now, and I have to carry out more repairs. I put the squeaky set on again, and I've no choice now but to get a set in Coleraine.

Stopping at a look-out point, I notice a low hill with some kind of monument on top. I climb up to find a flat stone with a compass embedded in a rock. It points to all the headlands and places of interests along the horizon.

Before heading off again, I join a couple at a picnic-table and share a packet of nuts. They're a mother and son from Canada. She's in her forties, and he's probably in his early twenties. She plays the harp and has been busking around the country. She's a laid-back sort of character and I soon learn that she's an atheist, like myself. We get talking about politics. 'It's a real shame – all the trouble. We've only been here a few days, but it seems so peaceful. It's hard to believe that thousands have died in such a tiny country. We've seen a lot of flags and paintings that must only incite hatred on both sides. A few towns have "No Surrender" signs on the highways, too. They should be banned because they only cause trouble. Peace is here now, and I think that though a United Ireland will come, it's a long way off. I honestly think all the churches here should be knocked or burned down – they cause too much bloody trouble.'

Back on the bike, the narrow unmarked road suddenly dips, revealing a winding descent to the coast. At the edge of a cliff, miles ahead, I see a Martello tower – another relic of the Napoleonic Wars. Beyond is Portstewart.

The descent is quite steep, and the brakes are well tested. I round a bend and into view comes a magnificent beach. According to the map, it's the nine-kilometre stretch of Benone Beach. It's rare to see a beach so vast. I park up the bike and take a stroll. Two young girls gallop past on huge chestnut horses. I want to stay here for the day, watching the waves breaking. It's warm and peaceful – until, that is, bikers dressed in studded black leathers and sporting curly moustaches arrive on the scene. In fairness, nobody gets hurt and they're remarkably polite – in fact, they're your stereotypical bikers: well-behaved and considerate.

Heading down the A2 towards Coleraine, I pass through the colourful village of Articlave. By colourful, I mean red, white and blue; it's everywhere. Every pole flies either the Union Jack or the Red Hand. I'm not surprised when a bright-orange tractor passes me out. I decide to give Articlave's pubs a miss because, honestly, I couldn't possibly listen to another Wolfe Tones CD.

Coleraine is jointed, and it's only Wednesday. My first stop is at a campstore-cum-bikeshop. The brakepads are my first concern, but I have no luck. A really helpful guy rings a few people and tells me of a website that does next-day deliveries. They're based in Ballyclare, near Belfast, and are guaranteed to have some. The only snag is that to get the overnight delivery, you must order before four in the afternoon. Now that it's after seven, it looks like I'm staying in Coleraine again tomorrow night. I'm not too pushed, and look forward to exploring the town.

The shop has everything else I could possibly want, and as I need a new stove – nothing fancy – I grab one for £20, and can't resist a cycle computer to replace the one I lost in the bog back in Connemara. At least now I won't have to work out my mileage from the maps.

At Safeways, I'm amazed at just how cheap everything is. Rip-Off Republic is right. Perhaps I'll move up to the North altogether. I pig out on chocolate muffins, custard-and-fruit cocktail, crisps and orange juice.

I book into Tullan's Farm Caravan Park, knowing that I can sleep-in tomorrow, and the only thing I have to worry about is how much custard to eat.

Day 23
There's a bit of a nip in the air this morning, and I'm in no hurry to drag myself out of my warm sleeping bag. I catch up on the news, and hear that the historic IRA statement is expected sometime today. Everyone assumes it will be a 'war is over' statement. I'd be very surprised if the IRA disbanded – that would surely only split the republican movement even further.

The centre of this university town is mostly pedestrianised, and every second building seems to be a bank. I'm not a keen shopper, but drizzle sends me wandering aimlessly down aisles of boutiques and electrical shops in an attempt to keep dry. I'm amused to see Celtic and Rangers calendars hanging side by side, but the bookshops seem to rigidly reflect the sectarian divide – or, specifically, the unionist or republican sympathies of their owners.

After a sandwich and a pint, I make my way to the library at the end of Queen Street to seek out an Internet connection and a copy of the IRA statement.

At the caravan site, I settle in for a quiet night in the TV room, and foolishly allow myself to be sucked into an eviction episode of *Big Brother*. Kamal gets voted out.

Day 24

Such efficiency. My brakepads arrive in the post. The rain in Coleraine continues to fall on my bike frame, so after sorting out the brakepads, I take the momentous decision to stay another day.

Day 25

The rest has done me the world of good, and I feel fit today and up for anything.

Traffic is a nightmare on the six-mile trip to Portrush, in County Antrim. Hoards of holidaymakers and hip surfers keep the town's amusement arcades and ice-cream parlours busy.

At midday, I arrive at what looks like the smallest train-station in the world. A tiny sign points to the Giant's Causeway cycle route, which crosses over the track and follows the railway line. I get talking to a half-dozen grey-haired tourists from across the Atlantic, and I'm impressed by their ency-clopedic knowledge of the railway. It's a three-foot narrow gauge, they tell me, and it runs between Bushmill's Whiskey Distillery and the Giant's Causeway. They seem utterly delighted to jump aboard the steam engine, and I make a start for the coast along the cycle path. As the train passes by, darkness sets in and I get an uncontrollable fit of coughing. It's as if I've stuck my head down the chimney of a Newcastle town house. I can hardly breathe and have to pull over to

127

allow this filth-spewing monster get well ahead of me before I'm asphyxiated. Still, you can't beat the old trains.

The Giant's Causeway is swamped with tourists – I've not seen anything like this since the Cliffs of Moher. It doesn't seem much at first, but after a few minutes examining the area alongside marauding groups of kids, I begin to appreciate this strange place. The 40,000 or so polygonal stone columns – arranged like steppingstones along the coast – are the handiwork of the giant, Finn MacCool. That's a fact, though boring scientists maintain that these basalt formations were formed around sixty million years ago by lava eruption. What nonsense. I'm extremely careful with my footing – with the steel plates on my soles and a weak knee, I could come a cropper any second.

I strike up a conversation with a group of teenage Chinese-Canadians. I'm dying to know what a Chinese-Canadian would think of the prospect of a United Ireland, but they haven't a clue what I'm talking about. The bravest asks if I'm in the IRA, but the rest look very unhappy, and the most timid of them explains that their parents told them not to talk about politics or religion while they're in Ireland. I'm sure they were also told not to drink alcohol, but that doesn't seem to have stopped them from stocking up on the cans of Carlsberg clearly visible in their knapsacks.

At the visitor centre, I'm tempted to buy a life-sized doll of Finn, but I don't think it'll fit on the bike. After filling my water bottles, I find a picnic table to set out my sandwiches and to test my new stove. I'm impressed with it at first – it lights easily and has an adjustable flame – but the water takes forever to boil.

It's mid-afternoon when I arrive at Carrick-a-Rede Rope Bridge. It's been in use by fishermen for over 200 years, and connects to a rock that overlooks the migration route for salmon returning to the north Atlantic. There's a steep descent to a tea-shop-cum-visitor-centre, and when I'm halfway down, a camouflaged speed ramp flicks my front wheel into the air. When it hits the road, the contents of my handlebar bag are tipped onto the roadway.

I pay an entrance fee at a little wooden hut, where the dear old lady behind the counter tries her best to persuade me to take out a year's membership of the National Trust. I decline her offer, and join the herds going and coming from the bridge. It's a bit like an unorganised migration of Caribou. I climb down a dozen or so slippery steps onto the bridge, and I'm a bit nervous as it sways left and right to the rhythms of a gobshite jumping up and down further along. I've crossed bridges like this in South America and Asia – some with frayed ropes and missing boards – but none had the character and setting of Carrick-a-Rede. A lookout point has views of Rathlin Island, where I intend to be tonight.

The migration back to the tea-room is far more demanding than the outward journey, with a tough climb up those blasted steps. Some caribou who can't make it are strewn about the ditches, legs in the air; some puff on cigarettes.

Back on the B15, heading east, I stop at another lookout point, this one with an interesting view of the rope bridge. As I take a few snapshots, I'm interrogated by a middle-aged Scottish couple as to what enjoyment I get from climbing these hills. They yammer on about cyclists not paying road tax and getting in the way of cars. Aside from being unapologetically anti-cyclist, I suspect they're also anti-black, anti-gay and anti-intellectual.

The cycling today has been up and down most of the time, but a few miles before Ballycastle I'm rewarded with a glorious descent into this charming harbour town. From here, a ferry will take me to Rathlin Island.

The next ferry is at six-thirty, which gives me an hour to relax in the town. I can't resist the aroma floating from a tiny fish-and-chip shop on the pier. Five or six women dressed in hygiene hats rush around behind a stainless-steel counter, taking orders and wrapping golden fish in white paper. Five or six impatient-looking customers grind their teeth, and it's impossible to know who's next or who's already ordered. A woman in front of me puts in her order and receives a ticket. A woman behind the counter shouts out numbers. It's a bit like a raffle in a community hall.

'Next.'

I give my order, but as I do so I'm confronted by an old-aged-pensioner waving her fist and who insists she was before me. I apologise. Apology not accepted, I'm almost pushed out the door by Supergran. Eventually, my turn comes and I study my numbered ticket – 083 – in a bid to memorise it so as not to get caught out. By now, the hungry crowd has swelled to a dozen or so, and it's like waiting to be called to jump out of an aeroplane. Will my number be next? Will it be the overweight Rangers supporter, the painter in his overalls, the farmer in wellies, the peroxide blonde with the large chest or the bollocks on the bike?

'Eighty-three.' Close to tears, I take my grub outside. A wooden bench by the door looks like a good place to sit, but Supergran is already there, gnawing at her fish as though she hasn't eaten for a week. Her Stone Age table manners are more than I can bear, and I make my way down the street, to a grassy park by the marina.

The forty-minute boat-trip takes me over the calm seas of Ballycastle Bay. Fair Head, the most north-easterly point of Ireland, can be seen rising 600 feet above the ocean. Technically, I'm surrounded by three countries, with the Mull of Kintyre in Scotland to my east, the Inishowen Peninsula of the Republic of Ireland to my west, and Northern Ireland to my south.

The seating arrangement is basic, with chairs spread around the deck in neat rows as though we're at a school play. One of the deck-hands checks the lock on a steel door, and gives me a serious look. 'Now, look here – don't you be opening that and jumping out, will you.'

According to my information, Rathlin is an *L*-shaped island with just over a hundred full-time residents – people, that is – and thousands of interesting birds at the RSPB sanctuary on the west side of the island.

The road out of the harbour can only be described as vertical. Even in San Francisco, I don't think I came across one as steep as this, and I have no choice but to push my bike up the hill. The summit reveals beautiful views of Church Bay, and I'm grateful to find the narrow road is devoid of cars. A few cyclists whizz by on rent-a-bikes, racing each other back to the village.

The cottages and farmhouses of Rathlin are hidden in wrinkles of land and surrounded by high basalt cliffs that plunge into the churning sea. The campsite is also hidden, and I stop to get directions from a strolling couple.

The campsite is run by Liam and Alison. Liam tells me to set up my tent on the grassy section by the house, and says Alison will call tonight or tomorrow for the fee.

My tent up, I mosey on over to the picnic table and introduce myself to my fellow campers.

Angela, from Belfast, is a teacher and artist who each summer for the past four years has rented a studio on the island. She's practically a resident at this stage. Tom, a professional photographer from west Belfast, is in his early forties. He's volunteered for a few weeks at the Kebble Nature Reserve up the road. Mark, an Englishman, is also in his forties, and judging by the 500 badges of puffins, kittiwakes and razorbills weighing down his woolly hat, he's an avid birdwatcher. He tells me that he's also a volunteer at the reserve. Yvonne, from Cavan, works as an artist in Belfast. Conal and Thomas – he's French – are both teachers in their early twenties.

Everybody here seems to get on like a house on fire, and Angela intends to fuel the flames with lots of wine and the suggestion that we light a campfire. She takes orders – I give her a twenty for a bottle of white wine – and off she goes in her little red car.

There's a great atmosphere here – it feels like I'm staying with relations rather than camping with complete strangers.

After a shower, I make my way to the bonfire at the first cow gate. Already, I've learnt that the island's geography revolves around cow gates, and that if you want to get anywhere on Rathlin, you must follow the cow-gate code. To get to the lake, for instance, you must go up the road, climb over the second cow gate on your left, and continue on down the field over the next cow gate.

Warming myself from the fire with the others – a glass of wine in hand – is pure heaven. It's dark now, and the street-lights of Ballycastle flicker on the distant mainland. When the wine runs out, Angela and Yvonne bring down hot whiskeys to keep us in high spirits.

I ask my fireside companions their views on a United Ireland. Tom – from west Belfast – says it won't happen. Angela, on the other hand, thinks it's demographically inevitable – Catholics will eventually outnumber Protestants.

We're having mighty *craic*, and then Angela makes a speech about the shortcomings of men. We put the fire out and hit the sack.

Day 26

My ferry leaves at eleven. But I'd like to get to know Rathlin, so I decide to stay another night.

After breakfast, Angela introduces me to Liam from across the road, and I pick his brain about the island's history. Its darkest period was around 400 years ago, when the English massacred every living thing. Women and children hid in caves, but were hunted out and beaten to death like seals. Liam tells me women were forced to remove their clothes before being pushed over cliffs to their deaths. It's a savage history, and he suggests I speak to Gus down at the boathouse visitor centre if I want to learn more.

I cycle up to the bird sanctuary to see how the hungover volunteers are doing. The reserve is located at the west lighthouse – a magnificent structure built practically halfway up a cliff. Steps lead down to an observation deck, with spectacular views of black basalt cliffs and sea-stacks thick with guillemots, kittiwakes, razorbills and puffins.

Tom is manning the telescopes focused on nesting birds, and busy dealing with the kids kicking the tripods and putting them out of focus. Mark is dealing with customers in the little hut.

Back at the campsite, I get talking to Niall – the fella who gave me directions yesterday. Turns out he manages Luka Bloom.

Angela's on the prowl in search of drinking partners for tonight, and Niall and myself go halves on a bottle of red.

Tonight's gathering consists of Angela, Thomas, Conal, Niall, his partner Etna, and myself. 'Give us an old song there, Etna love,' says Niall.

She has the voice of an angel: 'All around the blooming heather / Will ye go lassie go.'

'Look! Did you see that?' calls out Conal. 'Look – there goes another one!' Shooting stars blaze across the night sky.

133

Day 27

The head isn't the best today, but a cold shower soon brings me to my senses.

The tiny village at Church Bay consists of little more than a few shops, pubs and a hostel. The building that interests me most is the Boathouse Museum, where I'm told I'll find the historian, Gus. Outside the boathouse, there's a bit of a drama going on: two children are after colliding on their bicycles, and are bawling their eyes out.

Inside, a grey-haired man is telling a Yank about the 1917 sinking of HMS *Drake* by German torpedoes just off the island. Dates and details roll off his tongue. This has to be Gus. When the crowd is gone, I get a few moments with him and tell him about my trip and my interest in the history of the island. I buy a copy of his book – it's packed with the history of Rathlin – and I intend to post it to my friend Dominic back in west Cork, whose idea it was to visit this brilliant island.

At the pier, Yvonne is waiting for the ferry. We travel together, and in Ballycastle I say goodbye.

I chance a second visit to the chipper, knowing better this time where to stand and when to order.

The last few hours have been an almighty slog, but have yielded sensational scenery, including Scottish islands and the peaks of Mull of Kintyre only a dozen or so miles across the water.

When it's too dark to be on the road, I drag my bike and bags over a rusty gate, across a stream and over another rusty gate to a spot hidden behind some trees. The tent goes up, and despite wet feet and a few cuts from briars, I'm in good spirits.

Ian Paisley tries to put a damper on things by giving out stink to Tony Blair for scaling down the presence of the British army, but I turn the radio off and go to sleep. Sweet dreams, Ian.

Day 28

Carnlough. A man belts away with a hammer on a corrugated roof on some kind of boathouse. 'You're hard at it,' I say to him, only to get a keep-walking-if-you-know-what's-good-for-you look. Let's be honest – some of these loyalists hate us southerners.

In Glenarm, the oldest village in the Glens, an entrance gate to the village – I kid you not – is emblazoned with such welcoming slogans as 'No Surrender', 'Boyne' and 'Enniskillen'. The footpath, of course, is daubed in red, white and blue, and a representation of William of Orange on his horse hangs twenty feet above the street. I can't help wondering what they have to say about the possibility of a United Ireland, so I ask them. A little man walking a little dog up the street gives me a smile. 'How's it going?' I ask.

'You're not from these parts, are you?'

'I'm up from Cork. This place is beautiful,' I lie.

'You're right there.'

'Actually, I'm doing a bit of research. I think I know what you'll say, but – I hope you don't mind me asking – do you think there'll ever be a United Ireland?'

In fairness, the standard retort of 'No Surrender' is delivered without malice. Like many unionists, he seems convinced that if he keeps repeating this mantra, the border will stay forever.

The car ferry is pulling into Larne as I arrive, but there's nothing else of interest to report from this bastion of Orangeism. In fact, I feel I'm only going through the motions at the moment – cycling the coast but getting very little out of it. I consider popping over to Scotland for a few days, but decide to keep it Irish.

'I wish I was in Carrickfergus' – so the song says – and soon I am. But not for long. I head south for the city of Belfast.

135

Jordanstown Lough Shore Park is more of a prison than a camp site. Fenced in behind iron gates, the guy running the joint has given me my own set of keys. It's not a bad place, though – right on the shore, and only a few miles from Belfast city. Tomorrow, I'll be in the heart of the beast.

Day 29

After breakfast, I head south for an eight-kilometre trip into Belfast. There's a fantastic bike lane all the way, and I'm never more than a stone's-throw from Belfast Lough. People walk their dogs, cycle bikes or jog along, soaking up the morning sun and sea air. Retired men have colonised the benches, like the loitering teenagers they're always going on about.

At a post office, I borrow sellotape and a large marker from the friendly middle-aged woman working behind the counter. I use the envelope my brakepads came in – it's the perfect size for the book on Rathlin. As I write 'Clonakilty, Co. Cork', the friendly woman exclaims, 'Clonakilty – we were on holiday there last year – myself and my husband. What a beautiful place. Is that where you're from?' She tells me they visit her relations in Clon every year.

Her colleague – dressed in pink from head to toe – joins in the conversation, and I tell them all about the route I'm taking.

'Oh! You must write a book about it,' says the pink lady.

'I am.'

'You must tell us the name – we'll look out for it. What will it be called?'

'Well – the working title is something along the lines of *Will There Ever Be a United Ireland?*'

There's an awkward silence. A certain tension has descended on the place, I can tell. They seem to be hoping an armed robber will rush in, take them hostage and shoot the place up. Anything to distract from the appaling embarrassment I've inflicted on them. Both are lost for words. They look away from each other, and struggle to swallow lumps the size of golfballs. It's likely – I think later – that the visitor to Clon was Catholic, but her colleague in pink – and this has nothing to do with her choice of colour – was Protestant. Hence the awkwardness.

I'm standing in front of the blue and white 'Welcome to Belfast' sign, just off the motorway. I set my digital camera up on the tripod and use the self-timer. I take at least a dozen shots, with me running back to pose each time. I finally get one I like.

Across the Lagan River, the giant yellow cranes of Harland and Wolff dominate the east Belfast skyline. The shipyard was famous for its one-hundred-per-cent Protestant workforce, and for having built the *Titanic*. I get that sinking feeling.

I have a terrible map, but I know I must head west towards Donegall Square to find the Tourist Information office.

The forces of occupation patrol Belfast city centre. Goths, mostly. In fact, I'm wondering if I've happened across the annual clan gathering of the Addams Family, or perhaps Marilyn Manson is playing at the King's Hall. Angst-ridden teenage eyes stare out of sockets embedded in milk-white faces framed by the blackest of hair, blacker clothes, black-black fingernails, blackerest lips – I don't suppose the Black Hole of Calcutta was this black.

At Tourist Information, a helpful lad provides me with addresses for Sinn Féin, the DUP, the Ulster Unionist Party and the SDLP – no questions asked.

Heading up the Falls Road for the first time in my life, I'm excited by the prospect of meeting those most qualified to answer the all-important question – those who have lived with it every day of their lives.

On the Lower Falls, I stare up at the infamous Divis Flats. The British army took over the top two floors in the Seventies so as to monitor the movements of their enemies – specifically, every man, woman, child and suspicious-looking dog in the vicinity. In response to the IRA statement, the dismantling of these posts began only days ago, much to the relief of the local community. I saw a newspaper earlier with a smiling Gerry Adams standing in front of the flats as the work got underway.

At the Solidarity Wall, twenty-foot-high murals encompass a dozen different themes. The Irish struggle is depicted alongside that of the Palestinians, the Kurds and the Basques, to mention but a few. George Bush can also be seen here – he's sucking on a hose pipe that snakes into an Iraqi oil well, indifferent to the bones of dead Iraqis piled all round him. The hose is supported halfway by a well-animated 'British Support Hook'. A painting of Ciaran Nugent, the first blanket prisoner, also catches my eye.

The famous mural of Bobby Sands serves as a useful landmark for visitors seeking the Sinn Féin office. A plain, redbrick building, every window is protected with a metal shutter. The left entrance takes you into the souvenir shop, while the right leads to the office. I take the right. Inside, I pass through a glass security door. In a tiny hallway, a woman is speaking on the phone. She looks at me and raises a finger, keeping it raised in the air as she speaks.

When she hangs up, I explain why I'm here. She makes another call, and then tells me she's sorry, but nobody's available at the moment. 'Maybe if you call back in a few hours,' she says, though not convincingly.

Somewhat disappointed, I decide to check out the rest of the Falls Road. Black cabs and Celtic shirts are everywhere, but the most noticeable thing is the great community spirit. Everyone knows everyone. They wave to each other, honk their horns – everyone has a smile on their face.

I find a café and order a sandwich and a cup of tea, a watchful eye on my bike. A frail-looking man bends over to examine the rear suspension. While he considers taking it for a test ride, a bunch of teenagers gather around to discuss it. For some reason, those curious about my bike seem compelled to squeeze the brake levers. Sure enough, the boys each perform the squeeze test. Becoming bored, they head off to make petrol bombs.

Back at the Sinn Féin office, the same woman is still on the phone. 'Hello – Sinn Féin. Can I help you?' she says, giving me the finger again.

Within minutes, I'm explaining to Denis Donaldson, the press officer, what I'm here for, and he ushers me down a corridor into an empty canteen.

The Sinn Féin canteen is no different to any other canteen you'll find in the Western world. Dirty cups and half-eaten biscuits litter the tables, used teabags leak on the draining board, ashtrays overflow, and a picture of the queen with a dart through her eye is pinned to the dartboard. I'm sure the DUP canteen is much the same.

Denis is in his fifties – a short man with glasses and a very relaxed manner. 'Do you mind if I smoke?' he asks, pulling a cigarette from a box and lighting up.

'Ah! You're not back on 'em again, are you?' calls out a colleague when he enters the room. Denis raises his eyebrows but says nothing. The colleague leaves the room. Resting the cigarette on the ashtray, Denis claps his hands slightly, rubs them together, and says, 'Right – what can I do for you?'

I tell him about my cycle trip, and how I've been asking people their views on the prospect of a United Ireland.

'Oh yea – we'll get it alright,' he says with a wink, as if he knows something I don't know.

'Denis,' says I, 'it'd be great if I could ask Gerry Adams or Martin McGuinness the same question.'

For a moment or two, his eyes narrow to a sharp focus on something on the table – a grain of salt, I think. He's thinking hard. I know he wants to help me. He rubs his chin and looks up at me. 'It's a pity you weren't here yesterday. McGuinness was around. I don't know where Adams is today, but I do know they're all going to London tomorrow. Let me think.'

He sticks out his bottom lip as far as it can go, closing his eyes for a second – thinking. 'Wait – I know where Adams will be tonight.' He grabs a magazine and flicks through the pages. When he comes across the words, 'Féile an Phobail', he grabs his pen and encircles a section. Féile an Phobail is west Belfast's annual festival of music and culture, and includes *West Belfast Talks Back* – a question-and-answer session to be televised live from St Louise's College on the Falls Road at seven-thirty this evening. 'Adams will be there,' he says, pointing at the page.

We have a quick talk about the ongoing Loyalist feud that's seen murders by rival UVF and LVF gangs over control of the drugs trade and extortion rackets. He doesn't seem very disappointed by what's happening.

Outside, the BBC are preparing for an interview with Alex Maskey – one-time lord mayor of Belfast and now an MLA. Denis comes out onto the street, and we speak a little more. When a fella he knows comes along, Denis introduces me, telling him I'm from Cork. His friend speaks to me *as Gaeilge*.

'Oh! Gabh mo leithscéal; tá cúpla focal agam!' I splutter, before apologising for having only a little Irish. I feel ashamed for not being able to converse in my native tongue. It's fifteen years since I spoke Irish, and most is now forgotten.

'Ask him the question,' says Denis.

I do, and his friend is in no doubt. 'Oh yea – I'm certain we'll have a United Ireland.'

'But when?' asks Denis, as though he's as curious as me to know the answer.

'In about five or ten years.'

'That long!' says Denis, laughing.

I ask Denis if I might get a moment with Alex Maskey.

'Oh yea – he'll be fine with that,' he says.

I sit on a concrete bollard while Denis rests against the bonnet of a car with his legs crossed and arms folded. Alex Maskey give his interview to the BBC, while Denis tells me about the various attempts on Maskey's life. During one attack, he was shot at close range, and bullet fragments lodged near his spine.

After the interview, Alex walks over. A tough-looking cookie, he won seventy-one out of his seventy-five fights during his amateur boxing career – not a man to be messed with. I take out my dictaphone and ask him the all-important question.

'Alex Maskey – do you think there'll ever be a United Ireland?'

'Well, I'm absolutely certain of that. Now, there's no guarantee under the current political situation, if you know what I mean – under the Good Friday Agreement and so on. But as far as I'm concerned, a United Ireland is inevitable. We are working to make that sooner rather than later, and I think we can build a United Ireland in the not-too-distant future.' This is obviously not the first time Alex has answered this question.

'Good man – thanks for that,' I say, and I shake his hand.

Suddenly – from behind – rough hands grab my shoulders. Sinn Féin heavies unhappy with something I've said, I don't doubt. 'Paul! How the hell are ye?' I spin around to see Niall and Etna from Rathlin Island.

Alex and Denis take this opportunity to do a disappearing act. 'How come you're down here, Niall?' I ask.

'Oh, there's a fella giving Luka and myself a bit of a tour around the place.'

Niall introduces me to Luka Bloom. 'Oh! You're the fella from Cork that's cycling around Ireland. Fair play to ye. The acoustic motorbike is yer only man.'

I take a quick shot with my video camera, and Luka obliges with a blast of one of his songs. 'Pedal on / Pedal on / Pedal on for miles,' he sings.

Half-past-four. I order dinner from a pizza palace, and cycle back up the Falls Road to a quiet park I spotted earlier. I find a wooden bench by a playground and open my warm box. I'm starving. I'm not a fan of junk food, but today it tastes as good as Christmas dinner.

I keep a wary eye on a few drunks gathered under a tree, but I'm not overly concerned by their dirty looks and constant 'fuck-off' comments. What *does* concern me is the youngster walking towards me with a pistol pointed in my direction. Before I have time to react, he aims it at a tree and fires. Luckily, the eight-year-old is only armed with a toy gun. Well, I say toy, but it's actually a pellet gun, and I'm sure it's quite capable of killing someone.

He and his pal sit down beside me, cool as you like. 'Nice bike,' says the gunman.

'Thanks.'

'What's the pizza like?' asks his accomplice.

'S'OK, I s'pose. D'ya'wanna slice?' I'm pleased with my effort to speak their lingo.

'No thanks.'

They hang around for twenty minutes or so, and I can't get over how adult the conversation is. They're asking me questions like 'How are people treating you along the way?' 'How long will it take?' 'How do you manage for money?' I have to remind myself that these fellas are only eight, yet they sound like old men. I imagine the environment they're growing up in must accelerate their maturity, and they'll become adults before their time. I might be talking to the next Gerry Adams and Martin McGuinness.

At St Louise's Comprehensive College, an usher gives me permission to park my bike safely inside the porch. The doors aren't yet open, and the growing crowd is getting antsy. Another half-hour passes before we're let it, and I race for a seat a few rows from the front. Anxious photographers prepare for the entrance of Gerry Adams and the others, but Adams doesn't arrive. I don't know where Denis Donaldson gets his information from, but he seems to have been badly misinformed – Sinn Féin is actually represented by Conor Murphy. Sir Reg Empey of the Ulster Unionist Party, Dolores Kelly of the SDLP and the DUP's Arlene Foster complete the panel.

The question-dodging continues for a couple of hours, and is only enlivened by a few interesting comments from the audience. A woman complains about the PSNI making no effort to solve rape cases in her area. Robert McBride – a black South African – tells us he served time on death row for his activities in Umkhonto we Sizwe (MK), the military wing of the African National Congress, and that he's now a senior member of the South African police. His assertion that the PSNI is still a political police force is met with general approval from the audience.

Outside, it's pouring. This really is poor planning. I've now got to cycle eight miles in torrential rain to a campsite in Dundonald at the other end of one of Ireland's busiest cities – possibly its most dangerous, though Limerick and Dublin might have something to say about that – and it's already approaching ten o'clock.

Traffic is kind to me, with drivers giving me as much space as they can. I get lost a couple of times, and a sympathetic taxi driver waiting outside a posh hotel in his black cab puts me back on track with a shortcut to Dundonald. 'You're mad – you'll never make it tonight,' he says. Encouraged, I push off again into the dark rainy night.

By eleven-fifteen, I'm standing outside the locked gates of the Stormont Parliament buildings. The long avenue of Stormont is beautifully lit, and the huge building on the hill looks like a jewel as it glows green and pink in the night. It's fantastic, actually, but I can't seem to get my camera to capture the image the way it looks to the naked eye. Half a dozen blurry images later, I give up.

At Dundonald, a cyclist on a racer calls out to me as he goes past. 'Lost?' He's from around here, and is kind enough to escort me to the Ice Bowl – a disgusting leisure centre that mixes camping with ten-pin bowling and Indiana Land, whatever that might be. Distant church bells chime midnight as I squelch into reception. There's not a sinner in sight. Silence. As if time has frozen. Watching myself on a surveillance camera amuses me for a few minutes. A bewildered receptionist eventually comes to the desk, and I pay for the night.

The park is virtually empty. I set my tent up near the crazy golf, and ... zzz.

Day 30
Today, my plan is to call to the DUP office to see if Paisley is about, and to visit the Shankill Road. I'm a bit nervous as I expect some hostility somewhere along the line.

My first port of call is to an Internet shop in Shaftsbury Square, where I spend a couple of hours updating myself on what's happening in the world. It looks like the DUP plans to boycott any new discussions on restoring devolved government in protest at the British government's move to scale down security in the Six Counties. This announcement may mean that their office will be up the walls today, but I'll call there regardless.

Union Jacks alongside graffiti singing the praises of the Red Hand Commandos and the UVF leave me in no doubt that I've landed somewhere in the Shankill. An artist's impression of the Queen Mother on the gable of a red house does the woman no justice at all – I presume the intention is to honour her, not make her look like she's 155. If there was a competition for murals, Falls Road would win hands down.

The people here seem much older than those I came across on the Falls, or maybe it's pension day or something. For those not familiar with the geography of Belfast, I should point out that Shankill Road – a Protestant heartland – runs parallel with the staunchly nationalist Falls Road. The people of the Shankill are political prisoners of Sinn Féin, in that their local MP is Gerry Adams.

At a Shankill chipper, I'm served a wonderful kebab – not too spicy, just right. The plate is overflowing, and cheap too – only a few pounds – and I have to say that this is the tastiest meal I've had on my trip so far.

A frail woman enters the chipper, bent over and barely able to walk. The man behind the counter greets her. Melisa or Melinda, I think her name is. He leans over, asking her how she is today, raising his voice so the old dear can hear him. 'Who owns that bike with all the bags?' she shouts.

'Oh, that belongs to that big German over there,' he says, pointing to me. I nod at the woman, who carefully sizes me up with her squinted eyes. I keep up my undercover German pose for the remainder of my time in the chipper, and as I leave I'm given a send-off of little waves and smiles, and an 'Enjoy your trip,' from a young woman who obviously thinks my grasp of English is minimal. 'Ya, ya,' I reply, bowing my head.

I make my way down the Shankill, the object of stares and pointed fingers. Passing a fishmonger, I'm reminded of the bomb that blew up a fishshop on this very road back in 1993. In the window, a forlorn salmon lies rotting alongside its less illustrious cousins, and I wonder was it here the bomb went off. It was intended for a gathering of UDA commanders who had arranged a meeting for upstairs. But the meeting was called off, the bomb exploded prematurely, and ten people were killed, including the IRA bomber. I study the customers – an elderly woman jokes with the man behind the counter – and try to imagine the place disintegrating in a sudden flash of fire. What must it be like? Pieces of bodies and flesh stuck to the walls, a collapsed ceiling on the floor, rubble and dust, children screaming, pools of blood filling the cracks. Brutal stuff. The tragedy was naturally compounded by UDA revenge killings. As the German philosopher, Friedrich Nietzsche, put it: 'In individuals, insanity is rare, but in groups, parties, nations and epochs, it is the rule.'

I psych myself up with a view to quizzing the people of Shankill about a United Ireland. I know what to expect, but if only in the interests of balance, I should hear them out. I'll stick to my rule of five people. I walk my bike up the street, hoping the curious will break the ice for me. But they're not a very inquisitive bunch here, so I park myself outside a butcher shop. A well-dressed, elderly man with a walking stick is brought to a halt. 'Sorry, sir – I hope you don't mind, but I'm doing a little research on the views here about a United Ireland …'

'Are ye joking me? A United Ireland – no! I sincerely hope not. I can't see it ever coming about. Now, good day to you young man.'

That wasn't so bad. Two minutes later, an elderly woman gives me her view. 'No, and I'll tell you why. When someone has their family or friends killed – like many people I know – you can never forgive. It happens on both sides. They'll never talk to each other, never mind be in each other's company. For that simple reason, they'll never agree on anything. They hate the sight of each other and that's why there'll never be a United

Ireland. Even a lot of Catholics wouldn't want it.'

Meat hanging in the butcher's window conjures up nasty images of the infamous Shankill Butchers – a gang of UVF psychopaths that roamed this area in the Seventies. They abducted Catholics – many simply walking home at night – tortured and murdered them, normally by cutting their throats. The torture, even now, is unspeakable – suffice to say it involved knives and meat cleavers. Martin Dillon – author of *The Shankill Butchers* – estimates their tally at over thirty people. Many of the gang have been released from prison under the Good Friday Agreement, but it's argued that as they were actually serial killers – not 'terrorists' – they should never have been freed under the agreement. It's still early, so I'm hoping they're not up yet.

My unease outside the butcher shop prompts me to move further up the street, where I stop a young lad aged about fifteen or sixteen. He's a bit slow on the uptake, but eventually provides the predictable response. Negative.

My last interview on the Shankill Road is with a woman in her early thirties pushing a pram. 'Be careful asking that question around here. We're all unionists, and that question is a bit insulting. Cheeky, I think.'

I can't say I'm disappointed leaving the Shankill behind me. I never felt at ease there. The omnipresent Union Jacks and exaggerated – some might say hysterical – celebration of Loyalist culture reminds me too much of Nazism. I'm glad I went there, just the same, and I met some nice people. Hopefully, I've learnt something from the whole experience.

I've become familiar with the streets of Belfast these past few days, and my ride through the city and out towards east Belfast is surprisingly straightforward. I take photographs of the many murals displayed along Newtownards Road – UFF, UDA, KFC and the like – and eventually find myself outside the UUP office on Belmont Road. This should be the DUP office, and I double-check the address. I ring the door bell – maybe they can sort me out – but it's closed. A man in a white coat comes across the street to ask if I need any help. He's a butcher, judging by his outfit, or perhaps the men in white coats have pressing business with me. A helpful character, he tells me that the office is closed but gives me directions to the DUP office – a couple of streets away. He's delighted to learn I'm from Cork, as it's a place he's been to a few times – he has relatives near Kinsale.

I'm struck by how friendly the locals are towards me, and the community spirit here reminds me of the Falls Road.

The brick edifice on the corner of a side-street that houses the offices of the DUP makes Fort Knox look like a security risk. But it's still not what I was expecting. There are no sixty-foot posters of Paisley on the walls, and no souvenir shop.

I push the button on the intercom mounted on the heavy door. 'Hello. I wonder if I might speak to a press officer.'

Silence. I try again. Nothing.

More in hope than expectation, I push the door and can't believe my luck when it creaks open. Now I'm standing in a narrow hallway with high ceilings and a steep stairs to my right. The place is in a bit of a heap, with stuff scattered everywhere. Stacks of magazines and brochures are strewn about the place. Through an open door, I can see a dozen or so people dressed in suits and talking loudly on mobile phones. It's like a mini stock exchange. One of them I recognise as Peter Robinson, the deputy leader of the DUP. He's talking on a mobile – his far-away gaze gradually coming to focus on me and my orange vest. One of ours, he's probably thinking. Now this guy really has a lot to answer for. I remember an episode back in 1986 when he led an invasion of 500 loyalists into a County Monaghan village. They took over Clontibret garda station and held a military drill in the square. When his case came to court in Dundalk, republicans lay in wait, and I'll never forget the sight we saw on telly that evening of someone chucking a crate of petrol bombs at him and his minders as they fled the riot-torn town.

A red-haired man steps in between us and asks if he can help. Surprisingly, he takes the time to listen and shows an interest in my trip. He introduces himself as Simon Hamilton, the DUP press officer and a councillor in Ards. He beckons me upstairs to a quiet room, where he apologises for the mess, telling me that the new manifestoes are just back from the printer and need delivering.

I'm disappointed to learn that Ian Paisley isn't about, but Simon goes back downstairs to see if anyone else is available. I quietly prepare my dictaphone, hopeful that Peter Robinson will walk through the door. From below, I hear loud laughing. I have a feeling they're having a joke about the poor Paddy on the bike, or maybe Peter Robinson has just said he thinks there'll be a United Ireland within two years. Or maybe they're watching *Father Ted* – who knows, but I'm pretty certain it's me they're talking about.

Simon Hamilton comes back to tell me there's no-one available, but he'll answer my question himself. 'Well, as you know, we're a unionist party and we believe in the union between Great Britain and Northern Ireland. It's maybe easier to answer it from the perspective of my own lifetime and what I think will happen over the – God willing – fifty or so years or whatever I've left on this planet. I don't think that even by a basic numbers game – which sometimes you can crudely get down to – I just don't think those numbers are there in favour of a United Ireland. I mean, if you come from a basic position that essentially one hundred per cent of Protestants in Northern Ireland are in favour of the union, that gives you in excess of fifty per cent of the population that are always opposed to a United Ireland. There is also a small but significant proportion of Catholics in Northern Ireland who are actively opposed to a United Ireland. I think if there was a referendum tomorrow to keep the border, it would be carried with a massive majority, and I can't see the demographics changing in the long term. This pre-supposes we would have a right to vote on it. As you know, the principle of consent is there, where the majority must want to go into a United Ireland. But I suppose there's always a possibility that you could be forced in that direction. But I don't honestly believe that will happen. I believe there's too many problems, too many difficulties, and I don't think our own government would want to do that. The government of the Irish Republic wouldn't particularly like it either.'

I thank Simon for his answer. He tells me I'm a man of my word. I ask him why. 'Well, you said you wanted to ask me only one question, and that you did.' He walks me to the door.

Leaving east Belfast, heading back for Dundonald, I feel my job in Belfast is done.

It's just after six when I arrive at Stormont Castle. When I passed here last night, the huge black gates were locked, but now they're wide open, as though they're expecting me, so I cycle up the mile-long, rising avenue lined with uniform trees, immaculate lawns and antique lampposts. I don't bother to stop at the statue of Edward Carson, the Dublin unionist who stirred up a lot of trouble for the North and who dragged Oscar Wilde over the coals as a lawyer for the Marquess of Queensbury, who took exception to Wilde's relationship with his son.

The only signs of life here are the blue moving dots under the giant pillars at the front of the hall. As I walk up the steps of the enormous Parliamentary House, the dots turn into a couple of security guards. Dressed in white shirts, blue ties and big puffy rain-jackets, they stand outside the massive revolving doors. They tell me the building is closed to the public. They're both ordinary blokes – much like you'd meet at a football match or in the pub – very relaxed, hands in pockets. They're all questions about the bike and where I've cycled from. One of them kindly allows me a peep inside the revolving doors, where more guards stand alongside what looks like a metal detector. It's only a quick look but I thank him for it. Outside, the three of us talk for a few more minutes. I ask them what it's like to work in such a renowned place and to see all the famous – some would say 'infamous' – politicians and world leaders passing through. The modest couple say that after a few years working here, you don't really take any notice. It's a bit like any job, really. They wish me all the best on my trip as I freewheel back down to the gates.

Back in Dundonald, I share a bench with a friendly Dutch couple who've just set up their tent alongside mine. They've spent the last two days cycling from Dublin. Like most Dutch people I've met, they're easy to get on with and have a great sense of humour once they've loosened up a bit. I fill them in on cycling around the city, and they help me out with route options to Dublin.

Day 31
Friday morning. Today is my day off, so I'm going to do as little as possible. The last few days have been hectic. I've a lot of my journal to catch up on, and plenty of washing to do.

I subject myself to fast-food junk in the leisure park across the road, and waste a few hours watching families playing crazy golf and ten-pin bowling.

I'm in bed early – a little after nine – so as to get an early start for the beginning of the east-coast phase of my trip around Ireland.

Day 32

The morning is overcast and there's a nasty wind blowing. I'm on my way again, heading east along the A20 towards the coast. The road turns quieter as I connect onto the B172 country road into the little village of Millisle.

Millisle – over a dozen miles from Dundonald – lies on the east coast of the Ards Peninsula. A small village with little more than a few permanent caravan parks, it also has a long open beach that stretches for miles – a perfect place for breakfast.

People park their cars and take their dogs or husbands for long walks along the sand. I move my bits and pieces to make room on the bench for an elderly man with a hyperactive Jack Russell on a tight leash. We get chatting about the weather, sport, Al-Qaeda, a United Ireland. 'It'd make no difference to me. You still have to work hard all your life no matter who runs the country. But people are economically better off here, and I always like to consider myself British.' He tells me the Ards Peninsula is traditionally unionist with only a tiny minority of Catholics.

The A2 is monotonous and flat, but at least it's easy riding. After a few miles of pedalling through fairly average scenery, I arrive in Portovogie. I remember reading an article years ago about how they 'breed them hard' in Portovogie. The locals have pelted Sinn Féin and SDLP members with eggs when they came to talk about the local fishing industry, and they even called Paisley a traitor. They're not an easy bunch to please, and I've heard it said that differences of opinion between themselves are sometimes resolved with balaclavas and baseball bats.

The local hardware store must be doing good business in paint, as well as baseball bats, as virtually everything has been daubed with the red, white and blue of empire. Rangers jerseys hang from clothes lines, and I'm not sorry to say goodbye to Portovogie.

At Portaferry – on the southernmost tip of the Ards Peninsula – the clothes lines are draped with the green-and-white hoops of Celtic.

A young fella of about sixteen or seventeen is armed with a hurley and fires a sliotar against a wall in the square. He tells me about the friendly neighbours from Portavogie who sometimes come down in cars, drive around the square and shout abuse about Catholics. He says you couldn't wear a Celtic or GAA jersey up there. Even a Che Guevara T-shirt is taken as proof you're a Catholic.

The ferry that takes you across Strangford Lough from the Ards Peninsula leaves every half-hour, and soon I arrive at the harbour town of Strangford on the Lecale Peninsula. This patch of the Six Counties is famous for its lack of sectarianism. Apparently, even the Protestants play GAA here. It's a picturesque fishing village, but I'm not in a mood to dally.

Taking the coastal route for Newcastle, the next few hours are filled with easy riding on a beautiful summer's day. Open countryside with fields of wheat occasionally gives way to lovely coastal villages, including the original Coney Island – the one Van the Man sings so fondly of, not the one that features in every Hollywood fairground scene.

The Mountains of Mourne come into view, and that blasted song forces its way into my thoughts. 'La da da da da, na na na na na / Where the Mountains of Mourne sweep down to the sea / mmm, mmm, mmm, mmm.' Stop, leave my head, silly bloody song. Just when I think I've forgotten it, it surfaces again.

I'm still humming the tune when I roll into Newcastle. This resort town is the base for tourists exploring the Mourne Mountains (blast it – here comes that song again!), and this evening it's one big traffic jam. I have to take to the footpath. and though these busy family hang-outs are not normally my cup of tea, I have to say this place quickly grows on me. It's got a relaxed atmosphere and stunning scenery, and I cook up my supper on a picnic table by the shore of Dundrum Bay.

Replenished, I hit the road again. The flat A2 takes me on another coast-hugging adventure. Actually, there's no adventure, but the weather is mighty, the traffic is scarce, and I meander through the fishing village of Annalong and beyond Lee Stone Point, where the road turns inland to Kilkeel. Passing through the town, I take a wrong turn and get lost. I decide to follow the coast, but it's after nine, and I reckon I'll have to find a field somewhere. I'll worry about where I am tomorrow.

Just when I'm beginning to grow anxious about the lack of somewhere suitable, Sandiland's Caravan Park saves the day. It's a five-star jobbie, but I decide to check it out anyway. A young girl at reception tells me the place is full, and gives directions for another campsite down the road. I'm about to set off again when I'm surrounded by a gang of friendly teenagers. It's a mark of how lazy the kids are these days that cycling a bike can raise your status to just one notch below celebrity. The delay is fortuitous, because the woman who runs the place says not to worry – she'll find me somewhere to pitch my tent. She finds me a spot alongside a caravan, and then pops into the noisy neighbours to tell them to pipe down.

Comfy in my sleeping bag, I hear on the radio that Robin Cook has croaked. Can't say I agreed with all his politics, but I'd give him credit for his stance against the war. Pity it took him so long to wise up, though.

Day 33

On a bright, sun-kissed Sunday morning, I make an early start. My destination today is Crossmaglen in South Armagh, the heartland of republicanism.

County Armagh is the twelfth county I've passed through on this trip. At Camlough Lake, I jump over a gate to get a better look, and discover a bunch of youngsters swigging wine from plastic cups by the water's edge. My high-visibility orange vest leads them to assume I'm some sort of authority figure, but I can't say they look worried. I learn they've been on the piss since the night before – they're celebrating a birthday – and the party shows no signs of ending. I decline the offer of a vodka.

When you come across 'IRA' in metre-high letters nailed to a telephone pole, you know you're in Bandit Country. The British army came up with this nickname for Crossmaglen, and I gather that while some of the local lads are flattered, not everyone in the area appreciates it. In the Seventies, this was the town British soldiers most feared being sent to. (Basra probably has that honour now.)

> In Crossmaglen
> The fire burns true
> The patriotic flame will never die
> And when you hear the battle cry
> It will be the fighting men from Crossmaglen.

It's a song I heard many times blasting from the bedroom of a staunch republican with whom I shared a house in Holland. Seán had all the rebel songs. 'Oh go on home British soldiers / Go on home / Have ye got no fuckin' homes of yer own' was another one of his favourites.

Crossmaglen seems no different to any other town in Ireland

– not what I was expecting of this stronghold of resistance to British occupation. But the towering presence of Crossmaglen Barracks above the village square quickly reminds you that this is no ordinary town. The fort is wired up with antennae and all the latest video-surveillance equipment for listening to and watching every move of the locals. I remember reading about a study that found those living in Crossmaglen were three times more likely than the rest of the population to suffer brain haemorrhages because of the army's equipment.

No troops patrol the streets today, and no helicopters hover low in the sky, but not so long ago it was in-your-face stuff.

A pub just off the square beckons. It's a modern spot, with your usual bar and lounge, and God knows how many TVs. A bunch of rowdy young women are practising for a hen party, while the lads take the opportunity to watch a match. Waiting for my pint to be poured, I get strange looks from three men huddled at the end of the bar. It's not long before one walks over. 'I hope you don't mind me asking,' he says – and I can tell that even if I *do* mind he's going to ask anyway – 'but who are you?'

I have to laugh at such a brazen inquiry. Still, they can never be too sure around here, and I fill him in on who I am, my recent movements, my shoe size – pretty much the same stuff you'd have to own up to when quizzed by the Brits. Before I know it, I'm supping pints with Niall and his friends, and deep in conversation about the Kilmichael Ambush and the signing of the Treaty. Niall is from somewhere in Monaghan – only eleven miles down the road – and I get the impression one of the others is a local Sinn Féin councillor. Naturally, they're all happy to voice an opinion on progress towards a United Ireland. Niall says he'll never see it in his lifetime. The one I think belongs to Sinn Féin says, 'Yes, in about ten to fifteen years.' The other fella says we'll only have it when the British are crushed.

In the market square of Crossmaglen, I eat fish and chips as I read the plaque on the Phoenix Rising memorial, dedicated to those who suffered for their passionate commitment to Irish freedom. I have to move on to avoid the attention of a drunk. For a fella that can hardly walk, he seems keen for a fight.

After my last supper in the Six Counties, I say bye-bye to Crossmaglen and head the short few kilometres south into the Republic, passing the infamous Forkhill watch tower perched high on a hill overlooking Bandit Country. The British announced recently that they'll take it down. No-one's holding their breath.

At a crossroads with no signs, I know where I am. Vive la Republic. Thank God I've suspension on my bike, I think, as my journey resumes its course along the bumpy roads of the South. The N53 takes me directly into Dundalk town, a place I can't get out of quickly enough. It's nine o'clock, and I'm determined to make Drogheda within the hour.

A steep hill near Monasterboice demands extra effort, and I throw my weight onto the pedals. The back derailleur gets caught in the spokes and snaps, breaking the chain. This is bad news. All I can do is take a few links off the chain and cycle in single gear. It takes a while, but I eventually reload the gear and try again. I manage a few yards, but the chain is too loose. Back to the drawing board.

While I'm shortening the chain, a gaggle of teenagers arrive on the scene. I ask if there's a field around here where I can camp up, because now it's pitch dark and even if I could cycle, it's far too dangerous to continue.

'You can sleep in our bomb shelter.'

'Bomb shelter?'

'Follow us.'

The kids have colonised a bomb shelter attached to a blasting quarry – the workers used to take cover there when explosives were detonated. They lead me up the road for half a mile or so, and through briars and high grass. Their concrete cave is kitted out with half-broken chairs, and the whole scene is like something out of *The Famous Five*. But it'll do for me.

The teenagers head off, and I organise some grub and my sleeping bag.

Day 34

My night in a bomb shelter can be added to my list of weird and wonderful sleeping accommodations that includes the Great Wall of China, Copacabana beach, a bed with a head-hunter's daughter in Borneo, and a night strapped to a luggage rack on the roof of an Indonesian bus.

Drogheda is around ten kilometres away, and I've no choice but to push my bike there. Yet I'm in good spirits. It's another beautiful day, and I can't really complain, especially when I think of the poor bastards all over the world starting their day with a twenty-mile hike to fetch water.

My first brush with history today takes the form of the Monasterboice Dolmen. Or so I think, until I learn it was constructed way back in the dark and distant year of 2000 to commemorate the twinning of Monasterboice with some village in Scotland.

With a few miles and a fake dolmen behind me, I'm elated to see an endless downhill section that probably goes all the way into Drogheda town. Further on, I come across another fake monument: a high cross with the papal flag surrounded by hundreds of candles, flowers and bottles of holy water. It commemorates the visit of Pope John Paul II in 1979. Although I was only eight at the time, I still have vivid memories of the visit that brought Ireland to a standstill. We were all so innocent back then. He's dead now, and I shed not a tear on his passing.

John Paul would have been at home in Drogheda. Polish has become its second language. Construction workers with yellow vests and white helmets speak it. People selling tickets speak it. Young girls in shops speak it.

Castle-like buildings and stone gateways – there were once eleven of them leading through the old city wall – give the town a sense of history. Drogheda also seems to be over-provided with pubs and betting shops.

I get directions to a bike shop on North Quay by the Boyne River. A man who seems to know what he's doing tells me to call back in an hour and he'll know then what's required. If the part needs to be ordered, I might be in town a few days. He recommends the Green Door Hostel across the road.

What's behind the green door I wonder, as I walk the narrow corridor to reception. A bearded Metallica fan with the grandest Kerry accent you'd ever hear books me in. We chew the cud for a while: he tells me about his band, I tell him about my trip, he complains about the ridiculous number of new houses being built in his home town of Kenmare. Rob runs the hostel with a six-foot-something German with blonde dreadlocks, and who looks like she earns extra income as a nightclub bouncer.

'Well now, if I was shtaying here meself, that'd be the bed I'd take,' says Rob, pointing to the one in the corner.

I drop my gear and head off for a good fry-up in a restaurant across the river. The place is overrun by yellow vests and white helmets, but I don't see any Polish workers dining out for breakfast. I suppose it's hard to buy breakfast when you're on only a few euros an hour. It's simply incredible how, in this day and age, two people doing the same job, side by side, end up on different rates of pay.

Yer man in the bike shop tells me I need a part for the derailleur, and it'll have to come from Koga – the Dutch crowd that made the bike. He can order the part, but it'll take at least

159

a week. 'Leave it with me for the moment,' I say, holding back the tears. 'I'll try to get one myself.'

I find an Internet shop across from the beautiful St Peter's on West Street, but the bicycle websites bear no fruit, nor bike parts. I find a payphone and ring a shop in Dublin that sells Koga, but the man that deals with Koga is on holidays for three weeks, they tell me. Desperate, I ring Koga in Holland. I'm surprised and overjoyed, to say the least, when they tell me they'll post me the part straight away, and that I'll have it in a few days. Fantastic. They even wish me a pleasant holiday.

I'm in mighty form now, and can relax for a few days in this lovely Polish village. Back at the hostel, I strike up conversation with a Scot – Richard – who's lived in Ireland these past few years. He's in town to visit his good friend Dixie – a poet, he tells me, and a wheelchair-bound MS sufferer to boot. Richard is off to meet Dixie for a few pints, and invites me along.

We collect Dixie in Richard's BMW – the one he says he won in a poker game. We find a quiet pub near Laurence's Gate, and I wheel Dixie in. He's a bit of a celebrity here, and everyone seems genuinely pleased to see him. I'm a little uncertain about holding the drink to his mouth, but I soon get the hang of it. He recites a few of his poems, and though I'm not one for poetry, Dixie's compositions are spellbinding.

A few pints later, I'm back on the fags. The three of us go outside – me and Richard puff on a Benson and Hedges – my first in five years – while Dixie smokes a joint to ease his pain.

Back in the bar, a longtime friend of Dixie's – Denis – joins us. Denis had a terrible car accident seven years ago, but lived to tell the tale. It certainly didn't affect his sense of humour, and he looks none the worse considering what he's been through. A bit stiff he tells me, and he can only walk short

160

distances. He reminisces about Dixie and himself pheasant hunting in their early twenties. 'Ask Dixie about the time I shot two pheasant with the one shot – right through their teeth it went.'

Richard show off his Glasgow Celtic tattoo to a young lad dressed in the latest Celtic shirt. 'See that there, laddie. I don't have to be buying no fucking new jersey every year.'

A jazz band is at fever pitch, and the drink is flying in all directions. I get talking to a good-looking German woman in her forties who works in Swords. She's heading up to Belfast tomorrow for a day trip, and I promise to go with her. Dixie conks out in his wheelchair, and by now I owe Richard half a pack of smokes.

I forget how we ended up in Dixie's gaff, but somehow I find myself happily sucking on bottles of Heineken while a couple of pals of Dixie's – John and Paul – knock out tunes on guitars. The parrot flying around the room is Paddy. He's of the African variety, and for pure divilment likes to turn on the kitchen tap.

When chucking-out time arrives, Richard gives me directions back into town. Passing a 24-hour petrol station, I get a craving for another fag, and foolishly purchase twenty Benson. My relief at reaching the hostel turns to quiet despair when I discover I'm locked out. I spend three hours chain-smoking before a young Polish fella leaving for work lets me in.

Day 35

The head isn't the best, but I've had worse, and breakfast helps.

I'm not up to much, so I spend most of the day reading up on Drogheda. The Battle of the Boyne took place just down the road, but the darkest times were when Oliver Cromwell paid a visit in 1649 and organised the annihilation of around 3,000 people, including priests, women, children – in fact, anything Catholic. The governor of the town, Sir Arthur Ashton, was beaten to death with his own wooden leg. A hundred locals who hid in St Peter's Church were burnt to death when the soldiers set it alight. Drogheda's few survivors were shipped off to Barbados as slaves. It's sad to think that this bastard – the Lord Protector of England – died of natural causes. Worryingly, there's a new school of revisionist out there busily trying to play it all down: the likes of Kevin Myers, who reckon it's all been blown out of proportion. What a bollox.

Day 36

Richard arrives. Not Scottish Ricky with the BMW, but Bangor Richard on a pushbike. He's pedalled from Newry. A maths teacher, Richard is making the most of his long summer break by taking in some of the east-coast scenery. He's well up on history – especially Irish history – and the two of us and a couple of hitchhikers from the Basque country get deep into a discussion about ETA, the IRA and Herri Batasuna.

Our conversation is brought to a sudden halt by a new arrival. Six-foot-four, shaven-headed, combat boots – meet John Smith.

'I'm just out of the nick,' he boasts.

We say nothing. We don't have to, because he just flows with information. John is en route to Belfast for a court case. The SAS, it seems, are unhappy that he gave important information to Sinn Féin and the gardaí. But first he must visit Newgrange to 'talk to a few stones' and 'jump through some portholes' so as to prepare himself for the hearing. He produces legal documents that look one-hundred-per-cent legit. One refers to articles he wrote and pictures he published in a combat magazine. It's all headed paper with sophisticated legal jargon, and if they're fake documents, I'm highly impressed.

I spend the night with John. His size-twelve feet overhang a top bunk opposite mine, and I keep them firmly in view, hoping to Christ he has no more surprises in store.

Day 37

Metallica Rob presents me with a padded envelope decorated with Dutch stamps, and I waste no time getting the part to the bike shop. Within a couple of hours, I'm on the road again. Drogheda has been fun, but I can't see myself back there any time soon.

Two hours later, I'm back in Drogheda. I'd only managed ten miles before my gears jammed. Those clowns in the bike shop had put the chain on way too short. They admit their mistake and put on a new chain, but they're less than apologetic about the whole thing. Where the fuck's Oliver Cromwell when you need him?

The wasted thirty kilometres couldn't have come at a worse time. I started late today, and now I have to pedal hard. Taking advantage of the flat terrain and still air, I pass quickly through Balbriggan and into the lovely seaside town of Skerries. The tide is out and old fishing boats in need of a lick of paint lean against the stone-walled harbour. It's shallow at the edge of the harbour, and the seabed is littered with tyres, broken pipes and sheets of plywood covered in green algae. Families stroll the walkway by the shore, and people scattered on benches read books and newspapers or aimlessly stare at the horizon. All very innocuous, yet I can't help thinking that something's missing. Since I crossed the border a few days ago, I've noticed that the east coast lacks the friendliness typical of the west of Ireland. There's a different culture here – a cold and unwelcoming one. You get very few smiles, everybody sticks to themselves, heads down, and eye-contact is followed by a quick look the other way. There is an urgency here that is thankfully absent in the west.

Perhaps my sombre mood is informed by the fact that the next few hours will be spent navigating my way through the chaotic streets of Dublin city. At Swords, the very edge of the metropolis, a couple of wound-up Dubs in a Ford Escort prepare me for the horrors ahead: 'Get off the road and buy a fucking motorbike, ye bollocks, ye.' Delightful.

When I get lost, the day turns into the worst of my entire trip. Down a narrow road that's as busy as a highway, I'm hurtled savage abuse from impatient drivers. I keep to the left as much as I can, but for one besuited prick it's not enough, and he leans on his horn for half a minute. Now the meaning of road-rage becomes apparent. I'm ready to clobber some bastard.

I've cycled through crazy cities like Beijing, Saigon, Sydney, San Francisco, Cairo, Amsterdam and Rio, but never in my life have I met such a bunch of fecking morons. The Dubs might be the nicest people in the world, but today I've met probably every asshole that ever came out of the place. I'd love to hop on a bus and bypass the city of stress, but I can't – I'm in this for the long haul, right around the coast, no cheating. Emotionally, I'm at my lowest point since setting off more than a month ago. I push the bike along a footpath for a few minutes, just to get my head sorted and to calm down again.

The inner city isn't too bad, and the odd bike-lane and friendly foreigner improves my mood. *They*, at least, seem to have been reared with a little politeness – such a contrast with most of the Irish-born neanderthals I've run across today. An American and a German are kind enough to ask if I need directions when I stop to look at my map.

The city has changed so much from when I used to go

clubbing here a little more than a decade ago. I read lately how it's become one of the biggest weekend destinations in Europe. Why, I do not know. I could be anywhere in Europe right now – wish I was – and hardly know the difference between there and here. In Europe's widest shopping street – and no doubt its busiest – Daniel O'Connell seems to be crying from his plinth as he observes the rampant consumerism that has ripped through this city, and Jim Larkin seems to be telling everyone to fuck off. God only knows what damage the next two hundred years has in store. I'm supposed to be asking these people their views on a United Ireland, but I can't be bothered. Somehow, I don't think it matters to most of them if they're ruled by the Irish, the English or Ronald McDonald. A more appropriate question might be 'Will Ireland ever win the World Cup?', or 'What colour will be in next winter?', or 'Does my arse look fat in this?'

My intention when I began this trip was to stay in Dublin a couple of days, but now I can't get out of the place fast enough.

Not far from Dún Laoghaire, another warm welcome is shouted from a car. 'Getaway, yer langer, ye!'

Christ! That's it – someone's gonna get a kicking! I swing around in fury, only to find Niall Rynne leaning out from the passenger seat of a car. This man must be following me. First I meet him on Rathlin Island, then on the Falls Road in Belfast, and now he finds me in Dublin. What are the odds?

Niall pulls over and we have a laugh for a few minutes. I quickly fill him in on where I've been since Belfast and tell him what a shit day I'm having. He cheers me up with a present of Luka Bloom's new CD, and says he'd be happy to promote my book, if I ever write it. 'Say hello to Etna for me,' I call after him as he disappears into the city traffic.

The brief encounter has raised my spirits, and when I arrive at Dún Laoghaire Harbour just minutes later, I'm back to my perky self. I make use of the toilets in the ferry terminal, and get funny looks from people slouched in chairs as they wait for the next car ferry to whizz them across the Irish Sea – a trip I've made myself more than once.

It's been modernised since I was last here, but Dún Laoghaire still has much of its character and charm. Up Summerhill Road I go, and into the compact streets of Dalkey, home to the rich and famous, among them Bono, Enya and Neil Jordan. Great spot to live – if you've got a bottomless bank account or don't pay taxes. Some properties around here have five-million price tags hanging off them. I dunno would Bono allow me to camp on his front lawn tonight, like Tom in Donegal. I guess not. Well Bono, someday, bloody someday, even a beautiful day, with or without you, I'll find what I'm looking for, maybe where the streets have no name, but I betcha it'll be even better than the real thing, ye lemon, ye.

Mocking is catching, I think, as I'm faced with the hard climb up the steep Killiney Hill. At the top, I reward myself with a rest on a lonely bench. Commuters, shoppers, workers and drug barons whisk by aboard the DART that runs alongside the beach below me, and I thank my lucky stars I'm not with them.

It's after eight now, and a low sun hangs over the magnificent vista of Dublin Bay. It's the best scenery I've seen since the Glens of Antrim – some say it compares favourably with the Bay of Naples.

County Wicklow will tonight have the honour of accommodating me. A barley field on the road from Bray – the Garden of Ireland – to Greystones is where I'll rest my weary bones. I avoid damaging the farmer's crop by camping as close to the ditch as I can. My humble abode is a noisy spot as cars and the odd truck hurtle down the hill. My sleep is further disturbed in the early hours by a group of drunken revellers singing rebels songs; Bono and his mates, probably.

Day 38

The mood is good today. It's only just after six, but already traffic is busy. Busy birds going about their business from tree to tree put a smile on my face.

A 24-hour petrol station in the over-developed fishing village of Greystones sorts me out with a hot breakfast. After an unstimulating ride along the quiet R761 south, I pass through the village of Kilcoole – the setting for *Glenroe* – and take a detour to Ashford in search of the famous Ashford Castle. I feel like a right gobshite when a local tells me it's in County Mayo, and I try my best to hide the Cork accent.

A sign for Mount Usher Gardens on the River Vartry comes into view. Their famous collection of plants has been gathered from all over the world. But Ireland has been my own personal backgarden these last few weeks, so I give this little one a miss and push on through Wicklow town, with its sweeping beach and fine harbour.

It's been an easy ride so far, and Brittas Bay has provided a great view. But rain threatens as I arrive in Arklow just after noon. Suddenly, I'm dying for a pint; have to have one. In a sports pub on the main street, I meet a Wicklow lad – Anthony, in his mid-twenties – who's giving the local lads a hard time for watching soccer on the big screen. This hardcore Gaelic fan tells me how he spends much of his time travelling the highways and byways of Ireland by bus, working only when he has to. We both agree that life's too short to be breaking your bollocks everyday. We have a good ol' banter about politics, and he assures me there'll never be a United Ireland, as both sides up north hate the living sight of one another and will continue to do for years to come. 'No, not a hope,' he says.

Anthony gives me directions to Clogga beach, but as it requires me to negotiate a network of tiny country roads with few coastal views, I opt for the more direct N11 to Gorey town, in County Wexford. At a little village called Inch, I stop at a monument dedicated to the memory of Anthony Perry of Perrymount and Michael Redmond of Tinnock, both of whom fought for the United Irishmen in the 1798 rising. Anthony Perry – a colonel – was tortured by British troops using a method called 'pitchcapping'. This involved the pouring of boiling tar over the head and allowing it to cool. It would then be ripped off, along with much of the scalp. Perry was later hanged.

I don't hang around long in Gorey town. I seem to yearn for the countryside now – probably a continuing reaction to … well, I won't even say its name, but you know where.

My route for the rest of the day will be the R742 south to Wexford town. The weather has improved, and I can just make out the sun poking through the clouds. I haven't seen much of the Irish Sea since leaving Arklow, but that all changes when I land in a gem of a little fishing village called Courtown on the River Ounavarra. There's some sort of festival on here today. A live band by the pier is being enjoyed by hoards of holidaying families. I wash a few sandwiches down with a cup of tea while watching a mad group of kids jumping off the pier into the river. Dangerous, but highly entertaining to watch. We'll be seeing one of these young lads in the Olympics; somehow, he's taught himself to perform crazy summersaults thirty feet above the water.

Courtown is just one more place I'll have to return to some day. I certainly don't think it deserves its poor reputation.

At Ballygarret, I'm intrigued by a couple of plaques erected in the village. One – 'The Texas Connection' – commemorates the many Irish who left here to help in the colonisation of North America – specifically, Texas – where they did their part in the annihilation of Native American Indians. The second memorial – '1798–1998' – commemorates those from around here who resisted their colonial rulers and who made great sacrifices for liberty, equality and fraternity. Read it how you will, but the word 'contradictory' springs to mind.

Twenty or so towering wind turbines near Kilmuckridge serve as my next excuse for a break. A visitors' carpark has been provided, allowing me to get closer to these things than I've ever been before. Round and round they go, whirring gently in the breeze. They're a bit hypnotising, and have a strange attraction about them. But really, they're a blot on our landscape. After all, who'd volunteer to live within earshot of the constant whirring? Apart, that is, from the farmers who permit them to be placed on their land for €15,000 a year, per turbine. I'm not up on the science of these things, but I gather that they're not really the answer to the need for renewable energy. Renewable profits, yes – why else would they be springing up all over the place?

For some reason, Kilmuckridge is called Ford on one of my maps. Perhaps it's The Village Formerly Known as Ford – as Prince would put it. For a place in the middle of nowhere, it's surprisingly crowded. The shop is jammed and the sight of youngsters eating ice-cream gives me an awful craving for the stuff. So bad, in fact, that I end up getting two blocks of it. Yes, two blocks. That's enough to do a family for a week, but they're only a euro each, so why not live a little?

Now I'm wondering how in hell I'm going to eat the frozen ice-cream. Finding a suitable spot, I set up my cooker and saucepan and drop it in to thaw, much to the amusement of the dozen or so teenagers that have gathered around me. These yapping youngsters are no different to any others I've met on my trip. They're mad to know everything about me, about the bike, about where I sleep, and about why I'm melting ice-cream in a saucepan in the middle of the street. But now's as good a time as any to say how pleasantly surprised I've been by all the young people I've met along the way (bar the dickheads in Donegal); Irish teenagers, as much as I thought I'd never say this (perhaps it's all the ice-cream that's just frozen my brain) are actually the politest and most mannerly I've met anywhere in the world. That can only mean good things for the future, I hope.

With almost the entire east coast of Ireland behind me, I bring my day to a close in a caravan park just before Wexford town. Tomorrow, I'll cross the River Slaney, and then my trip will take a new course. Go west, young man, go west.

Day 39

I feel sick in the stomach as I cross into Wexford town over the longest bridge in the Twenty-six Counties. It's not the ice-cream I ate yesterday that's making me ill – though it's not helping. No, it's the thought of the bloody carnage that took place on this very bridge during the 1798 rebellion. An eye-witness account published in 1801 describes how almost a hundred Protestants were put to death by a method involving four executioners piercing the victim with their pikes – two in the front, two in the back, raising the screaming victim off the ground till the life had drained from them. Their corpses were unceremoniously tossed into the river.

More than a century earlier, I read, Cromwell massacred 1,500 of the 2,000 locals. Is there any place in the country that murdering bastard didn't leave his mark?

On a quiet Sunday morning, Wexford town is almost deserted. The sound of a milkman shuffling crates breaks the silence on the narrow North Main Street. A search for an open shop proves frustrating until I happen across one on the quay. I know it's early, but why is the woman behind the counter so grumpy? It's not my fault, is it? Still, her breakfast roll is the best I've had anywhere in Ireland – I'm assuming she hasn't spat in it – and I'm soon back for seconds. Her mood has improved, and now she calls me 'Lovey'. What's it all about?

Breakfast is taken on a bench located beside a statue commemorating Commodore John Barry, the 'Father of the American Navy'. Now, here's a guy who'd give his right arm for a United Ireland. He helped send the British packing from the US, and it's only a pity he wasn't able to get back home and send the Redcoats packing from our shores. A half-starved seagull is perched on his head, its pitiful stare fixed on my grub, and I'm persuaded to share the best breakfast roll I've ever had.

With directions from two Sunday-morning club cyclists, I'm soon on the R733 that passes through Wellington Bridge and Arthurstown on the way to the ferry crossing in Ballyhack. I help out a lost Dutch couple on bikes, sending them on the right road to Hook Head. This headland was made famous by Cromwell during his murderous tour of Ireland when, prior to an attack on Waterford city, he famously stated, 'I will take it by Hook or by crook.'

Crossing the River Suir on the ferry, I meet a group of happy motorcyclists making their way around the Irish coastline on Honda 50s for a charity called Canteen, which helps young children with cancer. They have a film crew with them, and take some footage of me for their documentary. They seem to be having mighty *craic*, though I can't help thinking that it's all a bit too easy as these sponsored events go. Still, it'll raise money for a good charity, and fair play to them.

Passage East welcomes me and my fellow passengers to County Waterford. The little stone harbour and quaint cottages owe their origins to the Vikings who settled here over a thousand years ago. It's a testing climb out of here, and the badly signed network of narrow country roads is confusing.

It takes an hour to find Tramore. What's going on here, I wonder. A banner welcomes me to the four-day summer racing festival. Horse racing, of course, for which Tramore is famous. The streets are packed, the fun fairs mobbed. There's money being thrown around everywhere. I throw the little cash I have at a chip-van, and get back a quarter-pounder. I'm usually a little afraid of quarter-pounders, but this one ain't half bad. I share the table with two elderly women. They're easy to talk to, and I take the opportunity to get their views on a United Ireland. 'Oh, I'd rather not say. But Mary, you might like to answer it.'

'No – it'll not happen,' say Mary. 'Patriotism doesn't seem very important anymore. It's too much money, money, money now. People hardly talk to each other anymore. It's all material things. They don't care about their country or religion anymore. It's all about the pocket.'

I get sand between my toes on Tramore's fantastic stretch of beach, but for a moment I wish everybody would disappear. Just one minute – that's all I need – but my wishful thinking doesn't stop the kids screaming, the frisbees flying or the incessant barking of the aggravating Jack Russell yapping at my ankles.

Peace and sanity are restored on the road to Dungarvan. Then I make the mistake of asking a drunk for directions. He's English, actually. He doesn't think a coast road exists, and even the yellow one I point out on the map must be a mistake. And Dungarvan is north, not west.

A few miles further on, I come across a dead magpie. The body is squashed into the tarmac like many I've seen this last month, but as I get closer I notice its head is still perfectly formed amid the tangle of its fleshy remains. As I slowly pass by, I feel there's something not quite right here. Then a shudder runs up my spine – as if someone has just walked over my grave. The bird blinks. Jesus Christ, it's still alive. Its pleading eyes look into mine as I come to a halt, hardly believing what I'm seeing. I know what I must do, and a nearby rock seems to have been placed there by fate. But fate or not, I make the cowardly decision to pedal on, hoping the next car will do what I should have done but couldn't. I'm overcome by a sense of guilt, and the image of those blinking eyes is embedded in my mind. Hope arrives a few minutes later in the form of a juggernaut hurtling towards me. I see the driver's face as he flashes past, and wonder will he be the executioner. Or will the suffering continue? And for how long?

The highlight of my day – of my entire trip, I would say – begins when I hit the pretty coastal village of Annestown and its deserted beach. This stretch of coast is known as the Copper Coast. For miles, the cliff-lined shore reveals stunning hidden beaches, coves, castle-like ruins, concealed caves and the odd remain of the nineteenth century copper industry. Its breath-taking views and remoteness rivals that of any part of Ireland, and as with so many other places in my country, I previously had no awareness of it. The hilltop view overlooking the pier at Boatstrand is one of those that can hold you in a soul-awakening grip all day. Sweeping cliffs and sandy shores enclose the sheltered pier. A terrier runs after a tennis ball thrown by excited children, fishermen work on tiny boats, and a couple paddle out to sea on white surfboards. Pure magic.

I bypass Dungarvan, taking instead the busy, uphill N25 to Youghal. The slow climb out of the bay seems to go on forever. Up and up, every corner revealing more climbing. I'm rewarded with fantastic views of the town and Dungarvan Harbour, but I'd prefer a good meal. An apple washed down with what's left in my waterbottle will have to do as supper. I'm starving now, and can't wait to get to Youghal for a good feed. The cross-country ride is easy, with good open road and a shoulder that's a couple of metres wide. Crossing the bridge over the River Blackwater a mile or two before Youghal, I'm into my home county of Cork. It's the nineteenth – and final – county crossing of my trip. A chip-van parked at the side of the road just over the bridge is like an apparition. I'm weak with the hunger, and I'd sell my soul for a drink. I don't remember feeling this bad on a bike since I had to pedal for 200 kilometres through the forty-degree heat of the Australian desert with only two tomatoes to keep me going. When I arrived at Pine Creek, I was almost dead.

Still some way from death, I order a burger and chips from the English chappy behind the high counter. The quirky van resembles the restaurant carriage of a train. They're about to shut up shop, so it's last orders please. I polish off the first burger and just manage to get another before it closes.

At a picnic table, a local man – Noel – doesn't hide his curiosity, and doesn't mind sharing a few details about himself. He's tells me how he's been up in the North a few times, and his story about driving down a street during an Orange Parade a few years ago sounds a bit hairy. It was by pure chance he came onto the march, and he remembers clearly the look of some who saw his Irish Republic number plates. 'God, you could really see the hatred in their eyes.'

'Do you think those same people will ever agree to a United Ireland?' I ask.

'I wouldn't be very hopeful about it, Paul. Perhaps when there's been peace for a few generations, but not yet.'

I ask the owner of the chip-van if there's a campsite around Youghal. He says I can camp on the grass behind the van. 'People do it here every other night, anyway,' he says. With the wrecked state I'm in, I'd lie down anywhere.

Although I've a room with a view – of the grey estuary – and it's not visible from the road, it soon becomes very clear that I'm camped in the middle of a public toilet. Several times during the evening, cars pull into the layby, brakes screeching. Men jump out, run behind the van for a badly needed piss, only to find moi, writing my journal. Most bellow with fright when they see me, some look confused and apologise, while others calmly go about their business with a look of a man's gotta do what a man's gotta do. At three in the morning, I'm woken again with 'Ahhh – ohhh – yaahhhhh. Jesus, that's better.' At least ten people – nine men and a woman – have used my bedroom as a jacks tonight. One fella was so close, I'm sure he must have pissed on the bike.

I'm woken again at five by a security guard shining a torch on the tent. 'Are you alright there? I'm just checking the area.'

'Piss off!'

Day 40

Last day. Home tonight. Cycling under the famous stone archway of the clock tower straddling Main Street, I look up to see it's just turned seven. Yet I'm struck by the sheer number of people pouring out of shops with fresh cups of coffee, pre-packed sandwiches and enough fags for a small regiment.

I know this old port town from my younger days, and even then the character of the town was obvious to me. Only, the character I cared about most back then was the one serving up the pint of Murphy's. Thankfully, I'm a bit wiser now (I think), and know there's more to a town than the four walls of its pubs. The walls of the old town are what gives this place its character – something recognised by John Huston when he chose to film *Moby Dick* here back in the Sixties. Walter Raleigh spent time here, which might account for all the cigarette butts littering the streets.

The N25 to Cork city used to be half interesting, but EU funds have been squandered on over-priced tarmac here, just as they have all over the country, and it's now a boring stretch of road connecting uninspiring places such as Castlemartyr and Midleton. I know I should take the beautiful coastal roads through Ballycotton and Cloyne, but I can't help but opt for the shortest way home. I've only €20 in my pocket, so it's essential I make Clonakilty tonight.

I bypass Midleton on the Owenacurra River – the home of Paddy and Jameson Whiskey – and take a turn off after the village of Carrigtohill (where my mother went to school) and head down the quieter R624 to Cobh. I cross over a beautiful stone bridge with the ruin of a castle at the other end, and I'm now on what's called the Great Island – one of Cork Harbour's three islands, each connected to the mainland by roads and bridges.

Now this is what cycling is all about: peace and quiet, no rush, salty sea breezes. The flat, narrow road hugs Cork Harbour all the way down into Cobh, a seaside village that wouldn't look out of place in France. Its layout is unique in Ireland, and the oddly painted houses are the only giveaway that this is indeed Éire. Under the British Empire's thumb, it was called Queenstown, but since independence it's been known as Cobh – a phonetic and quite unIrish spelling for 'cove', as the place was once known as the Cove of Cork. The majestic St Colman's Cathedral towers above the narrow streets, and a few ships are anchored in the harbour. The town is steeped in maritime history, as recalled by memorials to victims of the *Titanic* and the *Lusitania*, and to the hundreds of thousands – possibly more than a million – who left for America from this port.

It's not long after midday when I hop off the ferry at the other side of Cork Harbour. It's a short crossing, only a couple of minutes, and you'd nearly walk it if you had a big pair of wellies.

The single-street town of Carrigaline holds little pulling power for me. I spent a couple of summers here in my youth with my first-cousins; I seem to recall it involved days of Commodore 64 and falling off skateboards.

It's a pleasure to arrive in one of my favourite spots in Ireland: the harbour village of Kinsale. You cannot but like the place. The maze of narrow streets, the colourful buildings, the hidden pubs and seafood restaurants, the expensive yachts in the harbour – all the ingredients necessary to make Kinsale the picture-postcard gourmet capital of Ireland, the Monte Carlo of the south coast. Like Monte Carlo, it doesn't come cheap. Real estate here has gone through the roof, and every plot of land with a view is worth something close to the GNP of three or four African republics. Today, the clear turquoise sky and warm summer breeze is free for all to enjoy, and will be until some smart capitalist discovers a way to charge us for it. Must enjoy it while I can.

In 1601, Kinsale was the site of a battle in which English forces defeated an Irish/Spanish force. It was after this battle that the Flight of the Earls took place – a pivotal moment in our history. Everything went downhill after that.

I've about €15 left in my pocket, so I treat myself to fish and chips. I plonk myself down on a stonewall overlooking the harbour, and get to work on the grub. It's pure heaven here. Even the Harley Davidsons don't spoil it for me when they thunder past. I'm so happy, I treat myself to a '99.

There was a time when the crowds got so big in Ballinspittle, even the statue couldn't move. Yes, it's an old joke but a good one, and it sums up that moment of sheer folly back in 1984 when fervent Catholics swore that the statue of the Virgin Mary I'm now looking at could be seen swaying from side to side. They came down here by the busload, and in a classic case of crowd hysteria convinced themselves the statue was not only swaying, but waving to them. Quite a crowd has gathered today, and at first I think this must be still quite normal, but then I remember that today, 15 August, is the Feast of the Assumption of the Blessed Virgin Mary – hence the large crowd down on their knees and fumbling with rosary beads. I walk to the top of the hilly field across the narrow road from the grotto, and from here have a good vantage point from which to savour the atmosphere and witness the fundamentalists below. Something that sounds like 'Hail Mary, full of grace...' crackles from the PA system. The faithful mumble 'Holy Mary, mother of God ...' in response. It's certainly not a moving experience for me. Being God-less myself, I find it all amusing and a bit of an education. It reinforces my belief that organised religion is nothing less than brainwashing. But it's good to know that these people – all of us – can practice their faith openly and without having to look over their shoulders in case English soldiers are coming to butcher them.

At a nearby shop masquerading as a house, I purchase a litre of milk. I share a wooden bench with an Englishman and his son who have just cycled up the hill. They're both a bit shagged, as are the bikes they're riding. But they're in mighty form, and are having a good old time by the look of it, laughing and cracking jokes. In our conversation, my adventure comes up, and as this may be one of the last chances I get to ask strangers for their view on that age-old conundrum of a United Ireland, I pop the question to Dad. The gist of his answer is that he thinks it's demographically inevitable because Catholics will outnumber Protestants in the future. It has to happen, and he doesn't seem to mind.

The two lads head off towards Kinsale as I relax and rest my legs a little more, while daydreaming about my soft bed that I intend to sleep in tonight.

Re-invigorated, I zoom on. I'm anxious to get home so it's pedal to the metal, though I'll try not to break the speed limit.

Further west I'm given views of Courtmacsherry, a tiny fishing village at the opposite end of Courtmacsherry Bay. Judging by all the housing developments and caravans over there, you'd be forgiven for thinking that the village only sprung up last year. But coming from the area, I know that it's been here since the year dot. From experience, I also know that Courtmac has some great pubs, and the *craic* is mighty on a Sunday afternoon, sipping a few pints of the black stuff.

And if you should happen to fall into the harbour after too many pints, I'm sure their famous lifeboat service – the fastest in Ireland – will quickly fish you out and put you back on your high stool. Unfortunately, I won't be visiting today.

For the next few miles, I'm never more than a stone's throw from the bay on a narrow road with a low stonewall that leads me into the delightful village of Timoleague. Its most famous landmark – the Franciscan Abbey – was built over 750 years ago. The huge stone building makes for a lovely view as I pedal over the tiny bridge into the village. Like Courtmac, this is another good spot to spend an evening or an entire weekend soaking up the friendly atmosphere and whatever refreshment is handed to you across the counter. There's also plenty of walking and hiking to be done locally if you're feeling a bit lazy or too worn out to take up the energetic sport of drinking. Today, I'm feeling lazy myself, so I pedal on through the village, and get a few waves from the crowd gathering at the grotto for Mass.

Suddenly it hits me like a ton of bricks that my journey is coming to an end. I left Clonakilty forty days ago with the intention of cycling the entire coastline of Ireland, and now I'm only nine kilometres away from achieving it. Pedalling along the familiar road, I'm oblivious to my surroundings as my mind focuses on what I've achieved during my United Ireland bike trip. I'm in a dreamlike state as memories flood my mind. I've covered almost 1,800 miles (the distance from Cork to Moscow as the crow flies) of some of the most inspirational and breathtaking scenery you'll find anywhere in the world.

I've had thirty-nine nights on the road, thirty-five of which I spent in a tent. I've slept at the edge of cliffs, in eerie woods, on lawns, on white sandy beaches, in quiet country fields and noisy ones off dual-carriageways. I've pitched my tent in rundown campsites and barley fields, on the most south-westerly tip of Ireland and on the most northerly one. I've camped on off-shore islands, behind a chip-van and even in a bomb shelter. It's been a journey of discovery in which every second has revealed new sights and sounds. The characters I've met and the situations I've found myself in will provide memories for life. I've had the drinking company of hilarious locals in rural pubs, shared bottles of wine around campfires with interesting tourists, watched traditional dancing and listened to magical Irish music and the beautiful Gaelic *bróg* on off-shore villages. I've had strange encounters with people such as John Smith, who even now must be fending off his former employers, the SAS.

A few things I didn't want to see along my journey was a Dutchman shitting in a stream at the foot of the Glens of Antrim, a ghost in the ruin of a farmhouse in county Mayo, the snapped chain and broken derailleur on my bike in Monasterboice, my flat tyre in the woods near Sneem, the water bottles thrown at me by those gurriers outside Donegal town, and the dying magpie on the road near Tramore.

It's been the trip of a lifetime and a hard-won battle at times, especially over the hills of Donegal and other part of the west. I've a mindful of memories and legs like Seán Kelly's, and there's not too many can say they walked into the DUP office in east Belfast and asked them if they thought there'd ever be a United Ireland.

As my journey of discovery is only a couple of miles from the end, I have to put a little question to myself. 'Do I think there'll ever be a United Ireland?'

I've accumulated an enormous amount of knowledge from pedalling the political highways and byways of my own country. The antiquity and landscape of every town and village I've been through has served as a reminder of the brutality and barbarism underpinning life on this island. It's been battles and bloodshed from day one, and I don't hold much hope for the future. Of course, we're no different than any other country. It seems to be the way of the world. We are, after all, only human. But within our social existence as tribes and communities, we have developed an identity and a culture that is ours to defend and preserve. Colonialism is a dirty word here, and so is the name of the nation that imposed it upon us. We had every right to oppose our invasion, the Cromwellian genocide, rape, the dilution of our traditions, the abduction of thousands for the slave trade. I've been a republican all my life, and a Catholic until I was sixteen. In that respect, little has changed during my trip. I'm still an atheist who would love to see a United Ireland in the morning. I think it's a just cause.

Occupation, in my opinion, is at the root of our long conflict, while religion seems to be the vehicle that drives it. The issue of occupation is a tough one, and the unification problem needs to be sorted sooner rather than later. The religious side of the whole fiasco is fast becoming a joke and an embarrassment. But the few that still practice it are becoming insanely more extremist. The 'pro-life' and anti-gay crowd are as gung-ho and as misinformed as ever.

I respect all religions and beliefs. Personally, I have no problem with people that have imaginary friends. You can believe whatever you want – it's your own business – but when this imaginary friend drives you through life telling you to invade Iraq, telling you that you have the God-given right to own a piece of land, telling you to strap a bomb to yourself or commit genocide against a nation of non-believers – this is where it starts to get nasty and people die. I was a passenger in that religious vehicle for sixteen years, but finally decided to jump out before the imaginary chauffeur crashed the car.

Of course, on the bumpy road of life, there are other vehicles and road users to consider, with many coming at you from the opposite direction with their flags out the windows and horns blowing. If you decide to start walking, it's best to get off the road before you get hit. The huge SUV (Dubya edition) whizzing up and down looks nice and safe with its big bull-bar and side-impact doors. The people inside look fat and happy (except for the poor black ones jammed in the boot). Its paint job is fading now and dents are becoming more common as it pushes other users off the road. Something about the petrol station running low, I heard someone say. I wonder, though, will that roll-cage and fancy air-bag protect it when it goes over the 1,000-foot cliff around the corner. As a conciliation to us here in the Emerald Isle, at least the blasted thing won't be stopping anymore to get refuelled.

As religion is dying in the country, a more shocking and sinister system is taking over our fertile land. Materialism and its mascot the Celtic Tiger have now replaced the religious circus. Fair enough – we all need materials to get through life and need money to get them, but we work to live – we shouldn't live to work. Our lives are far too short and precious to be thrown away on accumulating unnecessary ornaments. Saying that, I'm proud of the fact that we in Ireland can choose to have or to have not (most of us anyway). You can live modestly and avoid keeping up with the Joneses, though the Joneses are unfortunately moving into everybody's neighbourhood.

Ireland has transformed itself nearly beyond recognition in a mere ten years, and throughout my trip I've witnessed rampant consumerism propped up by a six-day week and a smug smile. Some see the Irish economy as some kind of caterpillar turning into a butterfly, but I see it as a butterfly metamorphosing into a slug. I'm all in favour of a good economy and a good quality of life, but I'm not in favour of one that involves sacrificing yourself just to survive.

It's the rip-off culture and exploitation that gets me. Our prosperity scales have now tipped to the other side, and it's ready to fall over. Irish identity seems to be falling fast into an abyss of greed and the lust for more, more and more. And more if you can get it. For many, it's the only way to go, and it's so easy to farm out your kids to crèches.

I'm all up for a United Ireland, but do we deserve it? Will it make any difference at all? Will it be like winning the World Cup – years of hard work, training, long hours and dedication, eating and sleeping it, just to hold the cup high and kiss it, singing 'We are the champions.' The celebrations may last a night. And then what?

And are we that different today to our British counterparts? We speak the same language, have the same political system, share many of the same sports, eat the same shit food, drink the same beers, have the same sense of humour, watch the same television programmes, listen to the same music, read the same newspapers and drive on the same side of the road. Since 'Independence' in 1922, we've had an opportunity to shine and show who we really are, but decided instead to continue with our British moulding.

Surely we could have made an effort to incorporate our Irishness of old into our modern society? To restore and update the Brehon Laws which today are recognised as the most advanced system of jurisprudence in the ancient world. Work harder on our language and traditions, be proud of our Celticness and take a few tips from the west of Ireland on how they've preserved their identity.

It's not all about turning back the clock to pre-British times, but becoming more defined about who we are. We have a strong history and identity, but in modern times it's becoming a little scattered. Whether our Irishness today is only symbolised in theme pubs, St Patrick's Day parades or Celtic football jerseys, I'm still very proud to be Irish. But be warned – our mask is slipping. In the eyes of the world, our pub habits are becoming alcoholic, our Church is a haven for paedophiles, and our welcoming arms are seen as increasingly racist.

And what about a United Ireland? Will it come? Yes, I *think* it will and I *hope* it will, but I also hope it won't be a shallow symbol without an identity. Still, whatever it turns out to be, I'm sure it'll sell well in the souvenir shops.

Up ahead, I can just make out the familiar sign: 'Welcome to Clonakilty'.

Postscript

In early August 2005 – day 29 of my round-Ireland cycle trip – I met Denis Donaldson, a Sinn Féin press officer, in the Falls Road Sinn Féin office. Denis was friendly and helpful. Later that year – in December – Denis was unmasked as a spy for British intelligence (MI5) and the Special Branch of the Police Service of Northern Ireland. He left the North and took up residence in a pre-Famine house in County Donegal. In April 2006, he was shot dead.

The war may be over, but it seems the killing has yet to stop.

Paul Shannon
November 2006